D-Day: A Layman's Guide

D-Day: A Layman's Guide

Scott Addington

©Scott Addington 2014
All rights reserved

Cover Image: The US 4th Division, Utah Beach, D-Day, 6th June 1944.
By Jason Askew.

The right of the author to be identified as the author of this work has been asserted in accordance with the Copyright, Designs and Patents Act 1988.

All rights reserved. No part of this publication may be reproduced, photocopied, stored in a retrieval system, or transmitted in any form or by any means except as permitted by the UK Copyright, Designs and Patents Act 1988, without the prior permission of the author.

Other books by Scott Addington:

WW1: A Layman's Guide

WW2: A Layman's Guide

The Third Reich: A Layman's Guide

Waterloo: A Layman's Guide

The First World War Fact Book

Heroes of The Line

The Great War 100: The First World War in Infographics

Five Minute History: First World War Battles

Five Minute History: First World War Weapons

All books are available from Amazon sites worldwide.

Want some free WW1 stuff?
Visit www.scottaddington.com for more details!

Introduction

There are very few days that alter the course of history. There are very few days where people can look back and say, "There. That was the day when it all started to change."

6th June 1944 was one such day.

Seen by many as the single most important day in the twenty first century, 6th June 1944, or D-Day as it became known, was the beginning of the end for Nazi Germany. It heralded the beginning of a new chapter in the story of the Second World War. A chapter full of hope, a chapter full of struggle, but a chapter that would ultimately end in victory.

The day itself was epic beyond measure. The brazen plan of sending thousands of men wading up onto the beaches of occupied France directly into the teeth of the Atlantic Wall defence system was seen as optimistic by some, foolhardy by many and borderline suicidal by others. The top brass of the Allied Supreme Command thought the risk was worth it and went ahead regardless.

The invasion was years in the making, was intricate in its detail, masterful in its innovation and cunning in its deception. It was quite simply one of the most incredible military operations in the history of military operations.

Following in the style of 'World War One: A Layman's Guide' this short narrative is more like a chat down the pub than a heavy historical text. I have tried to make the story flow naturally but have not overloaded the reader with mountains of detail. The chapters are sharp and to the point, perfect for dipping in and out of whenever the fancy takes you.

The men that fought on D-Day showed the whole world courage beyond measure and this Layman's Guide is my attempt at telling their story in an engaging way that appeals to people that may not have read about D-Day before.

I hope I have done them all justice.

SMA
May 2014

Contents

Battered but defiant: "We shall fight on the beaches..."

Wolkenkuckucksheim: The Atlantic Wall

The decision to invade

Where and when? COSSAC

SHAEF and the friendly invasion

Intelligence and resistance

The fate of the Reich

Deception and deceit: Operation Bodyguard

Blabber-mouths and gossip-mongers: Letting the cat out of the bag

The Grande Plan

Invention and innovation: A technological invasion

Cancellation, frustration and nerves

Just six gliders: The pointy end of 156,000 men

Operation Deadstick: Pegasus Bridge

The Paras drop in

Mission Impossible: Silencing the Merville Battery

We'll start the war from right here: Utah beach

Bloody Omaha

Pointe du Hoc

Gold beach

On! On! You noble English! Sword beach

Payback: Juno beach

Operation PLUTO (Pipeline Under The Ocean)

Mulberry: It's a harbour, Jim, but not as we know it

Sit Rep: The end of the 'Longest Day'

Mix-ups, egos and politics: Why Germany failed to push the invasion back into the sea

References, sources and further reading

Battered but defiant: "We shall fight on the beaches..."

By the summer of 1940 German Blitzkrieg had conquered the majority of mainland Europe. Poland, Czechoslovakia, Denmark, Norway, Belgium, the Netherlands and France had all succumbed to the power, might and speed of the German Army as it bulldozed its way on to what seemed like inevitable 'total victory'.

Even the combined forces of the French Army and the British Expeditionary Force (B.E.F.) were powerless to stop the force of the German advance and they were pushed further and further back until they were finally trapped and encircled on the beaches around the French coastal town of Dunkirk. By 25 May 1940 the situation was so bad that almost 400,000 Allied soldiers were looking down the barrel of either certain death or capture. The decision to retreat across the Channel back to England was taken quickly and over nine days between 27 May and 4 June 332,226 men were successfully rescued from those beaches. It was deemed a stunning success, a miracle even, but British losses were 68,111 (killed/wounded/captured). Add these human casualties to heavy losses of material and equipment (243 ships, over 63,000 vehicles and half a million tonnes of general supplies, ammunition and rations) it all added up to being a very bad few days for British Prime Minister Winston Churchill.

On 4th June, as the final few thousand men were being brought back to England on a flotilla of small private boats, Churchill went to the House of Commons to report on the current status of the evacuation and consequent military situation. He, like the B.E.F., was battered but defiant and he spoke for an hour, concluding his address with one of the most famous passages of oration in British history:

"...I have, myself, full confidence that if all do their duty, if nothing is neglected, and if the best arrangements are made, as they are being made, we shall prove ourselves once again able to defend our Island home, to ride out the storm of war, and to outlive the menace of tyranny, if necessary for years, if necessary alone. At any rate, that is what we are going to try to do. That is the resolve of His Majesty's Government – every man of them. That is the will of Parliament and the nation. The British Empire and the French Republic, linked together in their cause and in their need, will defend to the death their native soil, aiding each other like good comrades to the utmost of their strength. Even though large tracts of Europe and many old and famous States have fallen or may fall into the grip of the Gestapo and all the odious apparatus of Nazi rule, we shall not flag or fail. We shall go on to the end, we shall fight in France, we shall fight on the seas and oceans, we shall fight with growing confidence and growing strength in the air, we shall defend our Island, whatever the cost may be, we shall fight on the beaches, we shall fight on the landing grounds, we shall fight in the fields and in the streets, we shall fight in the hills; we shall never surrender, and even if, which I do not for a moment believe, this Island or a large part of it were subjugated and starving, then our Empire beyond the seas, armed and guarded by the British Fleet, would carry on the struggle, until, in God's good time, the New World, with all its power and might, steps forth to the rescue and the liberation of the old."

This defiance in the face of huge pressure and disappointment following the evacuation of Dunkirk set the tone for the next four years. The Allies may be down, but they certainly were not out.

They would be back and would come back fighting... *"on the beaches"*.

The seed for D-Day had already been sown.

Wolkenkuckucksheim: The Atlantic Wall

Berlin, 11th December 1941. Adolf Hitler addresses the Reichstag with an eighty-eight minute monologue in which he announces to the world that Germany is now at war with the United States of America.

Not content with that small bombshell, the Führer also mentions for the first time his vision of making Europe an *"impregnable fortress"*. He went on to boast with much gusto that *'...from Kirkenes* (on the Norwegian/Finnish border) *to the Spanish frontier stretches the most extensive belt of great defence installations and fortresses...I am determined to make this European front impregnable against any enemy attack."*

It was a bold claim; the length of territory mentioned in this speech was the thick end of three thousand miles – that's a lot of fortifications. The line wasn't as extensive as he would like to make out either – indeed, at the time of his speech the Pas de Calais area of France, the area of coastline where most German staff officers expected an Allied invasion to occur, had precisely zero fortifications in place.

There was a lot of work to do if Hitler's dream of a fortified Europe was to become a reality, but Hitler was nothing but persistent, and he demanded that his generals build him the biggest, baddest defence system the world had ever seen. On 23 March 1942 Hitler issued 'Führer Directive 40' which, in anticipation of a large scale Allied invasion, stipulated that the Atlantic coastal defences should be designed in such a way so that any invasion attempt would be smashed to pieces either before the main landing force had a chance to reach land or immediately afterwards. He wanted 15,000 concrete strong-points manned by 300,000 soldiers, and as no one really knew where the invasion would occur, the whole of the coastline had to be defended. And by the way, the entire defence system needed to complete by 1 May 1943.

The man in charge of making the Atlantic Wall a reality was Field Marshall Karl Gerd von Rundstedt, a career soldier who came out of retirement in 1939 and after masterminding the successful flanking of the Maginot Line in 1940 that ultimately led to the collapse of France, was given the role of Supreme Commander: West, which ultimately put von Rundstedt in control of all of the occupied Western territories.

Thousands upon thousands of slave labourers, staff from the German state construction organisation (Organisation Todt), and civilian workers from the local population were forced to work twenty-four hours a day building the concrete fortifications, gun emplacements, pill-boxes and assorted other structures that made up the Wall. Eye watering amounts of concrete, steel girders and other raw materials were used up in the process. There were such chronic shortages of raw materials that parts of the French Maginot Line and the German Siegfried Line were dismantled and used to bolster the Atlantic Wall. The original deadline of 1 May 1943 came and went – it had always been an unrealistic target.

Towards the end of 1943 around half a million men were busy building Hitler's defence system. It was starting to take shape, but progress was still too slow. In the autumn, Field Marshall von Rundstedt asked Hitler for more resources to help finish the job. In response to this request Hitler sent Rommel.

On his return from Africa, Field Marshal Erwin Rommel had been given command of Army Group B, and with that came responsibility for the coastal defences of northern France. Rommel was also given an explicit directive to evaluate and inspect the coastal defences of the rest of the Atlantic Wall and report back directly to the Führer's headquarters with his findings. Seeing this as a move that undermined his authority in the region, von Rundstedt was less than impressed.

Rommel was not exactly jumping for joy with what he saw on his initial inspection either. He had spent the last few years fighting in Africa and hadn't set a foot in France since 1941. He had heard all about the Atlantic Wall and, like most of the German population, he was under the impression that it was a spectacular defence system that was pretty much completed and ready to knock any British and American invasion straight back into the sea. He was to be disappointed.

In Rommel's opinion, the Atlantic Wall was farcical; he even went as far as calling it a, "figment of Hitler's *Wolkenkuckucksheim* (cloud cuckoo land)".

Rommel was convinced that the invasion battle, and indeed the entire war, would be won and lost on the beaches. He knew that the best chance the German Army had of repelling any large scale invasion would be when the enemy was still in the sea, before they got any kind of foothold on land. He was known to say on many occasions that, *"The first twenty-four hours invasion will be decisive..."* With the backing of both Hitler and von Rundstedt, Field Marshal Rommel set about building a defensive structure that might have a chance to stop any invasion force in their tracks.

It was time to get busy.

On every beach that could feasibly handle an invasion force, huge numbers of anti-invasion obstacles were erected. These were an assortment of jagged sections of steel girders, concrete bollards and metal-tipped wooden stakes, many of which were adorned with anti-tank Teller mines or artillery shells that were primed to explode with just the slightest impact. These were placed just below high and low tide water marks and were specifically designed to rip apart troop-filled landing craft or at least delay them long enough to enable shore based guns to zero in on their targets.

In and around the beaches, especially the pathways that lead off inland, Rommel had his men sow immense minefields designed to stop the Allied force penetrating too far too fast. By the summer of 1944 approximately five million mines of various designs had been planted.

Behind these vast belts of ant-tank and anti-personnel mines Rommel's men took up their positions in the concrete bunkers, gun emplacements and pill-boxes. They were all linked together using underground tunnels and included offices, latrines, kitchens, water and ventilation systems and first aid posts. Thick belts of barbed wire and yet more minefields encircled these strongpoints in such a way as to funnel any attacking force into killing zones covered by machine-gun nests with interlocking fields of fire.

Every available artillery gun at Rommel's disposal was trained on the beaches and the sea. To supplement this firepower Rommel also used a few different offensive techniques, including rocket launchers, miniature robot tanks that could carry more than half a tonne of explosives via a remote control device, plus huge flamethrowers *(Abwehrflammenwerfer)* which could produce a sheet of flame almost 3m high and 4m wide. The flame was delivered via the touch of a button through pipes that were dug into sand dunes, making these weapons particularly nasty.

Further inland, great tracts of land were purposefully flooded to hinder enemy paratroopers. Any area within seven or eight miles of the coast that could be used as landing grounds for gliders were covered with large heavy wooden stakes nicknamed *Rommelspargeln* (Rommel's Asparagus). These stakes were booby-trapped with explosives and trip wires.

Field Marshal Rommel had organised the most hostile welcoming party ever seen. There was nothing left for him to do but wait for the inevitable. He knew the Allies would be coming. He just didn't quite know where or when.

The decision to invade

On 22 June 1941 the Wehrmacht smashed its way through the Russian frontier across a 500 mile front. The advance was staggering even by Blitzkrieg standards and Soviet losses were equally impressive. As Churchill publicly welcomed Russia into the arms of the Allies to fight in a common cause to defeat the Nazi regime the reply from Stalin was blunt and to the point. After more than three weeks' radio silence Stalin sent his first message to Churchill on 18 July 1941 demanding a second front be opened to help relieve the pressure on his own army.

The Allied Commanders didn't need a bunch of Russians to tell them they needed to launch an invasion of mainland Europe and thus open up a second front. They had been pondering it since Dunkirk. In October 1941, Winston Churchill told Captain Lord Louis Mountbatten to prepare for the invasion of Europe, explaining that, *"Unless we can go on land and fight Hitler and beat his forces on land, we shall never win this war."* On the other side of the Channel, the German top brass also knew that the fighting would eventually heat up in the west, hence the frantic building of the Atlantic Wall.

The question was not if there would be an invasion but when and where it would take place.

The US Army (more specifically its Army Chief-of-Staff, General George C. Marshall) were itching for a fight with Germany and were pushing for an invasion from as early as mid-1942. They even put together a full invasion plan: forty-eight infantry divisions would attack, of which eighteen would be British, backed up by almost 6,000 aircraft. These men would be dropped off by 7,000 landing craft somewhere between Boulogne and Le Havre. This would be backed up by a smaller invasion force consisting of ten British Divisions who would aim to occupy the Cherbourg peninsular. Everything had to be ready by April 1943; speed was of the essence here – in case there was a full collapse of the Russian Army. Churchill accepted the idea and the invasion plans were even given code names: 'Roundup' was to be the name for the larger invasion with 'Sledgehammer' the name given to the smaller British led attack on Cherbourg.

Despite Churchill's agreement, British Commanders hated the idea and regarded it as a suicide mission.

More pressure was heaped upon the Allies on 20 May 1942 when the Soviet Foreign Minister, Vyacheslav Molotov, visited Roosevelt in London. He passed on a message from Stalin that demanded the opening of a second front in France to divert a minimum of forty Wehrmacht divisions from his front line. This was bad news for Churchill, he wanted to keep Russia in the war at all costs, but he knew that any kind of mis-managed and hastily put together invasion would destroy his own fighting resources in a matter of weeks.

The Americans wanted to press full steam ahead with both 'Roundup' and 'Sledgehammer' but in a letter to Roosevelt, Churchill told him that, *"No responsible British General, Admiral or Air Marshall is prepared to recommend Sledgehammer as a practical operation in 1942."*

Instead of 'Sledgehammer' Churchill started to push for an invasion of North Africa as being a more viable second front, but just as the British top brass had hated 'Sledgehammer' the

American chiefs didn't fancy an African invasion too much either, so much so that there was a growing clamour for America to pull out of Europe all together and concentrate all her efforts on giving the Japs a hiding in the Pacific. Churchill had to act and act fast. That July, London was the venue for tough negotiations as Churchill aimed to convince his American colleagues that a North African invasion was the best solution in the short term and that he couldn't do it without them. Eventually Roosevelt rubber-stamped the proposals, but not before Churchill committed Britain to an eventual full-on cross-Channel invasion of France in the not too distant future.

One minor crisis was averted, but now Churchill had to convince Stalin that the second front should be in Africa and not France. After a dangerous flight which took him over the edges of the Barbarossa battlefield, Churchill landed in Moscow on 10 August 1942. As expected Stalin was not impressed with what he heard and even asked Churchill if the British were afraid of the Germans, however, he didn't really have much choice but to accept the Anglo-American decision to invade in the south.

Churchill had got his way and his 'soft underbelly of Europe' strategy was put in motion.

Another cog in the wheel of this strategy was an invasion of Sicily, agreed by Roosevelt at the Casablanca Conference in January 1943, although the American Chiefs of Staff continued to press their desire for a full scale channel invasion, in fact they only agreed to accept a Sicily invasion on the premise that operation 'Roundup' was initiated and seven divisions withdrawn for training and preparation. At the same time General George C. Marshall pushed hard for a date for the invasion of France to be fixed and agreed.

The date was to be 1st May 1944. The operation would also have a new code name:

Overlord.

Where and when? COSSAC

A couple of months after the Casablanca Conference, Lieutenant-General Sir Frederick Morgan was appointed to the post of Chief of Staff to the Supreme Allied Commander (this title was soon shortened to COSSAC). In late April 1943 Morgan and his COSSAC staff were given a three pronged brief:

Firstly he was to prepare a plan for a diversionary attack against the Pas de Calais to dupe the Germans into thinking this would be the main attack and encourage them to concentrate their defences in the wrong position. Secondly, he was to plan Operation Rankin, a quick and sudden cross-Channel attack of a smaller scale to help out Russia if needed or to exploit any perceptible weakness in the enemy. Thirdly, the priority role for COSSAC would be to begin preparations for *"...a full scale assault against the Continent in 1944 as early as possible."*

This was Operation Overlord.

Although Morgan, the head of COSSAC, was British his staff were a mix of American and British staff officers and this caused a few issues when they tried to get to work. The Americans were itching for a tear-up; they wanted to get as many guns, ships, boats, men, ammo, artillery and armour as they could possibly find, ship it all over to France and start giving Jerry a damn good kicking. And they wanted to do it now. The British, however, were a little more cautious and were not hugely keen on committing everything to this one single attack. Deep down they still preferred a war strategy that hinged on a Mediterranean offensive, rather than walking straight into France.

Meanwhile, Allied shipping was getting a pounding in the seas around Europe in the first months of 1943 from German U-boats. The dreadful losses were only stemmed after 'Black May' where the U-bootwaffe started to suffer heavy losses themselves. The damage had been done though and right from the off, COSSAC had to deal with a shortage of warships of all descriptions. If this wasn't bad enough the landing craft situation was already approaching crisis levels. Despite numerous engineering companies throughout Britain churning out as many of these boats as humanly possible, it was becoming obvious that acute landing craft shortages would limit the size and scope of any invasion plan. Indeed, the chaps at COSSAC worked on the assumption that they would not have enough craft for numerous landings over a wide landing zone; it would be more likely a three division assault, with each division landing side by side over a relatively narrow frontage. Not ideal, but they just had to get on with it. Things were not helped by the Americans limiting supply of landing craft from their own suppliers in the belief that if additional crafts were sent over to Europe they would be used in a Mediterranean campaign, something that they (the Americans) were deeply opposed to.

It was not a great start.

The overarching plan was to land troops as close to the ultimate objective (the Rhine-Rhur region of Germany) as possible; this would enable a quick and decisive advance without stretching supply lines to the limit. There were several options for a suitable seaborne landing site, all of which were considered in depth by the COSSAC team. Both the Netherlands and Belgium had a multitude of excellent ports that would be perfect for hosting an invasion, and they were close to Germany. Perhaps a bit too close though, especially to Luftwaffe bases which would put the invading troops under threat of repeated air attacks. Plus the low lying land in these regions was easily flooded which would make progress slow and costly.

Le Havre, in northern Normandy, was another region with a perfect port, but the Allied forces would have to land either side of the River Seine, which dominated that area. With two smaller landing groups, rather than one large mass of men, it would be much easier for the German defenders to throw any attack straight back into the sea. This, obviously, would not do. Brittany on the other hand looked perfect with Brest and other numerous ports offering ideal landing areas. However it was simply too far – both from Britain and the ultimate objective of the Rhine/Rhur. Cherbourg was closer to both, but the proximity of the German held Channel Islands, plus the exposed nature of the geography, meant it was a tempting option, but not tempting enough.

The Pas de Calais area was perhaps the most obvious choice due to its close proximity to Britain across the Dover Straights. Indeed on paper it was an ideal location in all aspects except one: because it was so perfect for an invasion it was where the German defence system – the Atlantic Wall – was at its most formidable. It was simply too dangerous to land large numbers of men directly into the sharpest teeth of the German defences.

Thus, by a simple process of elimination, all eyes settled on the Calvados coast of Normandy.

On the face of it this particular part of France had many advantages. There was the port of Caen; and there was an airport, Carpiquet, situated just outside of Caen which could prove very beneficial to the assault, especially if it could be captured early. This area was also relatively weakly defended (compared to the area around the Pas de Calais region) by the German Seventh Army which possessed just one Panzer division. Also the beaches in that region were open, sandy and had numerous roads or paths exiting off of them making the job of getting off the beaches after the initial landing very doable.

Everyone at COSSAC nodded and pointed to this part of France as being their preferred location for the invasion of Continental Europe. There was just one tiny question that needed to be answered. There was history of significant coastal erosion in this area and there were rumours that underneath all that sand was a layer of peat, if this was true it could dash any invasion plans as any large vehicle such as a tank would simply sink through the sand and into the peat. The big question that needed answering was this: could the beaches in this region cope with tanks, trucks, bulldozers and other heavy vehicles that would be needed during the landings?

There was only one way to find out, someone had to go to those beaches and collect samples.

That job fell into the laps of No. 1 Combined Operations Pilotage and Beach Reconnaissance Party, namely Major Logan Scott-Bowden and Sergeant Bruce Ogden-Smith who swam ashore to take samples of the sands on a beach that would later be given the code name 'Sword'. It was New Year's Eve 1943. Disembarking from their midget submarine, Scott-Bowden and Ogden-Smith swam ashore carrying various small arms and a dozen twelve inch test tubes. As they crawled along the sand taking samples, noting the location of each sample on waterproof writing tablets, they were careful to keep within the high tide mark so the water would wash away their footprints. As they collected their samples they could hear the local German garrison singing as they celebrated the impending New Year.

The results of the tests on the samples were good. The sand would be able to cope with the heavy traffic of an invasion force. The invasion was on.

Throughout January, Combined Operations Pilotage and Beach Reconnaissance parties revisited the Calvados coast, taking photographs and making notes of enemy defences, whilst back in Blighty Morgan and the rest of the COSSAC staff got busy drafting up invasion plans. By the time Eisenhower arrived in London to take control of the planned invasion, COSSAC's thoughts and ideas were relatively advanced. Eisenhower and his staff agreed with almost everything that COSSAC had planned, the only difference was that Eisenhower insisted that the invasion front be wider than planned to include a total of five Divisions.

Everything had been agreed, the invasion of mainland Europe would be aimed at the Calvados coast with the American forces landing to the west whilst British and Canadian forces would land towards the east of the invasion front.

For the team of invasion planners, it was time to get to work.

SHAEF and the friendly invasion

The choice of an overall leader for the Allied forces was always going to be tough decision to make. National politics, strong personalities and massive egos were always going to make such an appointment very difficult, and they didn't disappoint.

Churchill had resigned himself to the fact that any leader would be an American. The fact that the US Army would represent almost 75% of the total invasion force made this a simple inevitability, but who would be chosen to lead the men into the fight? President Roosevelt was leaning towards giving the top seat to General Marshall, he was very keen to give Marshall the opportunity to command the army he had trained in live combat. General Marshall had transformed the US Army from a small group of men totaling just 170,000 in 1940 to an army that was over seven million strong in 1943 and the best equipped and most formidable fighting machine on the planet. Churchill however was having none of it and dismissed the idea out of hand.

The only other US General who was considered to possess the required qualities to lead an entire expeditionary force was General Dwight D. Eisenhower. Eisenhower was at least a known quantity and had a good track record in leading invasions – he had commanded three of them already in the war, all of them involved British and American land, sea and air forces. He was also well respected by the British high command. He was, on paper at least, the perfect man for the job. On 7 December 1943 Eisenhower met with President Roosevelt in Tunis. It was here that the President turned to Eisenhower and told him the news. "Well, Ike, you are going to command Overlord." Eisenhower replied, "Mr. President, I hope you will not be disappointed."

The decision was made almost by default. General Dwight D. Eisenhower would be the Supreme Commander Allied Expeditionary Force.

Almost immediately Eisenhower returned to the US for a short break and several weeks of never-ending briefings and high-level strategy meetings. Simultaneously there began an energetic search for the most gifted commanders and leaders that could support Eisenhower. British Air Chief Marshall Sir Arthur Tedder (Commander-in-Chief of Allied Air Forces in the Mediterranean) was nominated to be Eisenhower's deputy. Admiral Ramsey who had masterminded the Dunkirk evacuation as well as the recent North African invasion was appointed as Naval Commander and Air Marshall Sir Trafford Leigh-Mallory was given responsibility for the Allied Tactical Air Force.

Perhaps the most important appointment would be that of Ground Force Commander of the Allied Armies. This person would be responsible for getting the men off the beaches safely in the face of a full on German counter-attack. Eisenhower desperately wanted to appoint Field Marshall Harold Alexander, the British General who had done much to solidify Anglo-American operations in North Africa, but Churchill didn't want to move him away from his current position on the Italian Front. Second choice was General Sir Bernard Montgomery with American Generals Omar Bradley and Jacob Devers commanding the US 1st Army and the US 12th Army Group respectively.

With all of the seats at the top table accounted for, Eisenhower returned to London in mid-January. On 15 January 1944 he sat down at his desk for the first time as Supreme Commander Allied Expeditionary Force.

It was game on.

Originally the Supreme Headquarters Allied Expeditionary Force (SHAEF) was located in the centre of London but Eisenhower quickly relocated the HQ to a more quiet area on the outskirts of the capital, in Bushey Park. Very quickly a canvas town was created and SHAEF quickly grew into a large and complex machine with six separate sub-divisions:

G1 – Personnel
G2 – Intelligence
G3 – Operations and Planning
G4 – Supply
G5 – Civil Affairs (establishing political control in liberated countries)
G6 – Psychological Warfare and PR

The tent village that was constructed for this purpose was nicknamed Widewing and by 1944 boasted some 750 officers and over 6,000 staff members all working towards one unified goal: achieving a successful seaborne landing on the Calvados coast and the subsequent liberation of France and the rest of Western Europe.

Easy.

The quiet suburb of Bushey Park was not the only part of the British Isles that was witnessing a 'friendly invasion'. Since January 1942 almost one million American soldiers had arrived in Britain as the build-up and momentum for the invasion gathered apace. Between the US and British Armies it seemed that the whole island had been taken over by the military machine. Every wood was crowded with military vehicles, every piece of flat land had been turned into a makeshift airstrip, tent villages sprouted up like mushrooms all over the south of England and every port and harbour was crammed full of naval ships of all shapes and sizes.

Your average American G.I. was awash with perceived luxuries such as cigarettes, chocolates, fruit and of course cash. They were paid much more than their British counterparts and as such tended to dominate the British social scene, crowding into bars, restaurants, theatres and other 'venues of entertainment' (some offering performances of a more adult nature). With such an influx of fit, vibrant young men with exotic accents flush with money, energy and spare time, many young British women had the time of their lives!

Intelligence and resistance

If Operation Overlord was going to have any chance of success, the chaps at SHAEF needed to know two critical things: the topography of the invasion beaches and the surrounding areas immediately inland and the nature and relative strength of the German defences in and around the chosen invasion area.

This was no small task, but the Allies did have two intelligence tricks up their sleeves that gave them a distinct advantage: firstly, by 1943 those clever chaps at Bletchley Park had cracked the German Enigma electronic encryption machine and were regularly intercepting enemy messages that relayed information about unit strengths and position, ammunition requests, defence placements along with more trivial messages such as those from Field Marshal Goering requesting that the Luftwaffe personnel he was going to visit and decorate that day be properly de-loused.

These deciphered messages, along with reports and messages received from the French Resistance on the ground meant that the Allies had a pretty good idea of what the Germans were up to. All they needed now was as much detail as they could possibly get on the landing areas, but so as to not alert the enemy as to exactly where any invasion would take place, the Allies embarked on a massive reconnaissance campaign that basically took in the entire coastline of Belgium and northern France.

Hundreds of high-level reconnaissance flights took place up and down the French shoreline, carried out by RAF and USAAF pilots captured every inch of coastline in exquisite detail. When these pictures were enlarged, spotters could work out rock formations as well as currents and tidal movements. To complement these high-level missions, RAF Spitfires flew at extremely low levels taking detailed panoramas in an effort to gain intelligence on beach defences, obstacles and any fortifications that were either complete or under construction. Such low level flying was extremely dangerous but these photographs gave everyone a great opportunity to analyse the beaches and get an advanced preview of what they would be seeing come invasion day.

All of these photos, all of the messages and reports from the French Resistance, all of the intercepted messages from Enigma filtered down to a group of professors specialising in subjects such as geography, geology and economics as well as professional draughtsmen and photographers who had set up camp in the Ashmolean Museum in Oxford to try and get their collective heads around all of this information. This specialist group, called the Inter-Services Topographical Unit (ISTU) had been set up by Winston Churchill in an effort to give any invasion force as much information as possible as to where they would be going. They even roped in the BBC who broadcast an appeal for photographs, postcards and other pictures that British travellers and holiday makers had collected on their travels to France. After an intense PR campaign the chaps at ISTU in Oxford were drowning in almost ten million pictures donated by the public.

All the maps, plans, documents and briefing notes pertaining to the invasion were marked 'Bigot'. This classification was even more secret than 'Top Secret' and only the privileged few were able to eyeball papers labelled 'Bigot', those with such special clearance were labelled as being 'Bigoted'. This odd code name was derived from the phrase 'To Gib' which had been stamped on the papers of the officers destined for Gibraltar. They would subsequently take a leading role in the invasion of North Africa in 1942.

By 1944, thousands of members of the French Resistance were working overtime to send a continual stream of information back to London and on to Oxford. The Germans knew they were doing it and even tried to deceive the Resistance into thinking defences were better than they actually were. It failed miserably. During May 1944 over 700 wireless reports and 3,000 written memos were sent to London reporting on German military dispositions. One such report, from a Resistance raid on German army headquarters at St. Malo, uncovered a detailed report on the Atlantic Wall by none other than Field Marshall Rommel. Among other things the report listed all the new beach obstacles that had been installed along the coast line and those that were due to be installed over the coming weeks. It was clear that although the Atlantic Wall was far from perfect, it was becoming more impressive by the day under Rommel's watchful gaze. This was backed up by reports coming in from RAF reconnaissance flights that showed the Normandy coastline bristling with all manner of obstacles and mines, not only on the beaches but inland too.

RAF Spitfires did their best to harass and hamper the construction of the German beach defence system. Low-level sorties were continually sent over to France to shoot up the German soldiers as they worked in the sand. Meanwhile the strength of the Resistance grew stronger, but so too did the German determination to crack down on any information leakage. The Gestapo became increasingly active and visible in all of the possible invasion areas. In the Pas de Calais and Normandy regions especially, it was becoming more and more difficult and dangerous to pass on any information across the Channel.

With such an increase in defensive activity on the part of the Germans, plus the heavy crackdown on members of the Resistance, it was obvious to the Allies that the Germans knew something big was about to kick off. But how much did they really know?

SHAEF began to get very nervous about the whole thing.

The successful deception tactics utilised during the recent Sicilian landings (Operation Mincemeat) had convinced SHAEF that a similar ruse would be needed to try and kid the Germans into thinking the landings would take place somewhere else along the coast. The relatively small scale of the Mincemeat deception would not cut it this time though. No. The stakes were infinitely higher and called for a seriously cunning deception plan...

They called it 'Operation Bodyguard' and it was formally approved on Christmas Day 1943.

The Fate of the Reich

Across the Channel, Adolf Hitler and his cronies knew very well that the Allies were busy plotting an invasion of some sort or another. They just didn't know where or when.

During a meeting at The Bergof, Hitler's Obersalzberg mountain retreat, on 20 March 1944, the Führer addressed his Western Front Army Commanders:

"It is evident that an Anglo-Saxon landing in the West will and must come. How and where it will come no one knows. Equally, no kind of speculation on the subject is possible. Whatever concentrations of shipping exist, they cannot and must not be taken as any evidence, or any indication, that the choice has fallen on any one sector of the long Western Front from Norway to the Bay of Biscay, or on the Mediterranean – the south coast of France, the Italian coast or the Balkans."

For all of his many failings, Hitler was an astute tactician. He knew that the Allied top brass were busying themselves with the planning of a large scale invasion, but he was also well aware that those same planners and plotters were spending a great deal of time, money and effort in an attempt to mislead him and his military leaders about the where, the when, and the how of said invasion.

And he would be correct.

He was also under no illusion that once a landing was made it was 'do or die' for both sides. It really would be a pivotal battle, and perhaps decisive in foretelling which side would eventually win the war outright. He was confident of repelling anything the Allies threw at him, but he was well aware of the gravity of the situation and didn't hold back his views.

"Once the landing has been defeated it will under no circumstances be repeated by the enemy. Quite apart from the heavy casualties he would suffer, months would be needed for a renewed attempt. Nor is this the only factor which would deter the Anglo Americans from trying again. There would also be the crushing blow to their morale which a miscarried invasion would give.

It would, for one thing, prevent the re-election of Roosevelt in America and, with luck, he would finish up somewhere in jail. In England, too, war weariness would assert itself even more greatly than hitherto and Churchill, in view of his age and illness and with his influence on the wane, would no longer be in a position to carry through a new landing operation."

He concluded his address by impressing on his commanders that, "On every single man fighting on the Western Front...depends the outcome of the war and with it the fate of the Reich."

No pressure then.

The big questions of when and where the invasion would take place occupied the greatest German military minds of the time throughout the spring of 1944. In Hitler's opinion it was simply down to gathering good intelligence...

Deception and deceit: Operation Bodyguard

Towards the end of November 1943 the 'Big Three' Allied leaders (Joseph Stalin, Franklin D. Roosevelt and Winston Churchill) got together in the Soviet Embassy in Tehran, Iran, to discuss the progress of the war and decide future strategy. It was during this conference that Churchill turned to Stalin and said:

"In wartime, truth is so precious that she should always be attended by a bodyguard of lies."

And so was christened Operation Bodyguard. It would be the most elaborate, the most intricate and the most daring military bluff ever undertaken. If it worked, it would be simply beautiful. If it didn't work then those chaps landing on the beaches of Normandy in the summer of 1944 would be walking headlong into a whole world of trouble. There was no option. It had to work.

Operation Bodyguard needed to achieve three separate deceptions: firstly it had to disguise the geographical point of the invasion. Secondly, it had to confuse the enemy as to when the landings would take place. Finally it had to try and convince the Germans that the actual full-scale invasion was in fact a diversion and the 'real' invasion force would be landing somewhere else.

Simple.

Thus Operation Bodyguard was implemented with gusto. It was a vast scheme that contained thirty-six subordinate plans. Because they could monitor German encrypted communications, SHAEF knew that the Germans were expecting the main attack to be aimed at the Pas de Calais, so it made sense for a large chunk of the Bodyguard bluff to keep this illusion rife in the minds of the enemy. This would keep the bulk of the German forces (especially their Panzer Regiments) huddled around the Pas de Calais for long enough to allow a strong beach-head to be formed in Normandy.

To help the Germans continue to believe Pas de Calais was the main focus for the attack a huge project was launched called Fortitude South. To make Fortitude South credible, a huge ghost army, the First US Army Group (FUSAG) was built, and in an effort to give it further credibility, it was given a real life (and suitably high profile) commander in the shape of US General George S. Patton. In an effort to completely con the enemy into believing this was a bona fide army with invasion intent, the Allies had to create authentic army radio traffic and 'produce' an actual army so it looked like the real deal to any enemy reconnaissance aircraft that went looking for FUSAG.

To do this, a group of 'real life' army radio operators spent weeks studying the radio traffic of authentic army groups stationed in England and then re-created it, down to the last detail, as being sent by FUSAG. The radio messages were purposefully made easy to decipher and made numerous mentions of invasion.

To add to the ruse, the Allies worked closely with the British and American movie industries and teams of special effects experts got busy building dummy planes, tanks, guns, jeeps and any other equipment a major invasion force would need. The 'make believe' vehicles and equipment were not perfect replicas, and were obviously dummies if viewed up close, but viewed from a long distance, by for example, a German reconnaissance aircraft, they looked the real deal. Leaks to the press added to the reality of FUSAG and some of Britain's finest architects were employed to create a huge but completely fake oil dock at Dover. The King even 'inspected' this phony dock and when the Mayor of Dover 'opened' it he made a speech celebrating the "opening of a new installation, the precise nature of which must remain secret until the war is over..." The RAF patrolled constantly over the area as if they were protecting it and if ever this dock was hit by enemy bombs, fires were started by massive sodium flares.

The Germans were quickly fooled.

At the same time as the deception in the south, another operation, nicknamed Fortitude North kicked off in Scotland. This operation mirrored Fortitude South in so much as there was another fantasy army in place, this one was positioned and primed to invade the coasts of Denmark and Norway. No physical dummies were created for Fortitude North as the Allies decided that no enemy plane would get so far north without being intercepted by the RAF. Instead this operation relied on mis-information being delivered to the enemy via false radio traffic and double agents.

The real difference between the two 'Fortitudes' was that the northern operation failed to goad much of a reaction out of the Germans who hardly noticed the buildup of 'forces' in Scotland in an effort to threaten the Nordics. In the south, however, the enemy had largely taken the bait.

Another component to the overall Operation Bodyguard was a slightly more successful Operation Zeppelin which was designed and implemented to convince the Germans of an imminent threat to the Balkans. It was designed to take advantage of an area of the front that Hitler himself thought very vulnerable, following a similar pattern a ghost army, this time the British 12th Army, was invented and shown to be preparing for a large scale invasion in the area, specifically Crete or Romania. As this area provided a third of the Third Reich's oil such a movement quickly came to the attention of Hitler became very interested very quickly, especially as Romania, Bulgaria and Hungary were beginning to get increasingly twitchy as Russia inched her way towards them. In an effort to bolster this front, Hitler moved three divisions away from the west to reassure his nervous friends.

Operation Bodyguard would never had been as successful as it was if it wasn't for the network of agents and double agents that drip-fed the enemy with information and mis-information in the months running up to the invasion in a brazen attempt to confuse and deceive the enemy. In another sub-campaign to Bodyguard (Operation Ironside) the Allies wanted to amplify German concerns about a potential invasion around the Bay of Biscay. Operation Ironside was carried out solely by double agents. A South American agent, codenamed 'Bronx' had been sending the Germans information for a while and had built up a significant level of trust. On 29 May 1944, just a week before D-Day, she sent a coded telegram that managed to get the attention of senior German panzer officers located in that specific area of the German Reich:

'Send £50 immediately. I need it for my dentist.'

The £50 indicated that the place of invasion was the Bay of Biscay and the subject of the dentist suggested the date of the attack. Did Ironside work? Well, the mighty 17th SS Panzer Division which was stationed in the Bay of Biscay area was not mobilised until 7 June 1944, one day after D-Day, providing a vital window of opportunity for the invasion forces.

Then came Operation Copperhead, another cunning plan aimed at fooling the Germans into thinking there could be a significant invasion towards the south of France. This plan used Lieutenant Meyrick Edward Clifton James of the Army Pay Corps who happened to look uncannily similar to Field Marshall Montgomery. A plan was hatched in which James would impersonate Monty in a propaganda film that would show 'Montgomery' travelling through Gibraltar and Algiers shortly before D-Day. The purpose of Copperhead was threefold: to make the Germans think that Monty was out of the country and thus there was no imminent invasion. To make the Germans think that when the D-Day fleet did set sail it was just a normal exercise, and lastly to pin down the four armoured divisions that were stationed in the south of France in case Monty was plotting something fruity for that region.

It was an extravagant ruse, and evidence suggests that it did little to sway the Germans in believing that there would be any significant action in the south of France.

The final act of Operation Bodyguard was played out on D-Day itself. Hitler and his staff were convinced that the Pas de Calais would be the destination of choice for the invasion party and as such refused to release reinforcements to help out in Normandy for several hours after the landings. When Allied intelligence discovered that the Germans had captured American orders showing Normandy to be the main focus of the invasion and they were now pushing large numbers of troops into the area, Bodyguard kicked in once more and using double agents passed word to the enemy that the captured orders were themselves part of the deception and the Pas de Calais was still the main target.
By the time Hitler realised there would be no second invasion the Allies had managed to get ashore and were building up forces quickly to meet the expected enemy counter-attack.

The greatest bluff in military history had worked beautifully.

Blabber-mouths, honest mistakes and near disasters: letting the cat out of the bag

Operation Bodyguard may have worked out beautifully for SHAEF, but on many occasions the Germans were gifted opportunities to find out the truth but failed to take advantage of the situation.

Numerous breaches of security took place, giving the chaps at SHAEF multiple coronaries. Leaving top secret documents on trains or in the back of taxis is not a modern day phenomenon as proved by the British Staff Officer who left his briefcase in the back of cab. The briefcase contained the entire communication plan for Operation Neptune, the naval portion of Overlord. This was indeed a potentially devastating faux pas, but luckily for this particular officer the cabby was an honest chap and took the case straight to the nearest lost property centre.

With only a few days to go before the actual invasion, an old army friend of General Eisenhower could contain his excitement no more and declared to all and sundry in the dining room of Claridges that the invasion would happen before 15 June. This particular American official quickly became an ex- friend of General Eisenhower and he was promptly demoted and sent back to America to think about his indiscretion. Another American soldier, Sergeant Thomas P. Kane, who happened to be of German descent and worked in the Ordnance Supply Department of SHAEF, sent a bundle of classified documents to his sister in Chicago by mistake. The parcel actually spilled its contents over the floor of a Chicago sorting office and duly sent the Allied military authorities into panic mode. Although everyone involved was stringently interviewed and investigated and SHAEF accepted that it was nothing but a genuine error, everyone and anyone who could have possibly seen any part of the documents was kept under close surveillance until after D-Day.

The biggest scare came on the night of 27/28 April 1944 during a full scale rehearsal of the landings by American Troops. The exercise was codenamed Operation Tiger and took place on Slapton Sands in Lyme Bay due to their similarities to the invasion beaches 'Omaha' and 'Utah'. Unknown to the practising troops, German E-boats were patrolling in the area and sunk a number of tank landing crafts with the loss of some 650 men – either killed or drowned. This loss of life was a complete disaster but it was when it was discovered that ten 'Bigots' (the code name given to personnel who had been given special access to invasion information of the highest sensitivity) were missing, the people at SHAEF got very jumpy indeed. If any of these 'Bigots' were captured by the enemy there was suddenly a very real possibility that the plans for the invasion of Europe had just become fatally compromised.

Although the exact date for D-Day was not known by anyone at that time, not even Eisenhower, they all knew the exact locations of the various invasion beaches – if the enemy got their hands on that information it would be an utter disaster, and there was a very real possibility one or more of them had been taken prisoner. Divers were sent to search the wreck sites to look for bodies and collect identity tags. To the huge relief of the Overlord planners, all ten bodies of the 'Bigots' were successfully recovered.

On 3 June, one of the biggest journalist errors in history occurred when the Associated Press actually announced the invasion across five continents during a practise run for an anticipated invasion special announcement:

URGENT PRESS ASSOCIATED NYK FLASH:
EISENHOWER'S HQ ANNOUNCES
ALLIED LANDINGS IN FRANCE

Luckily this release was recalled quickly enough to stop it making it into any of the written press.
The risks to the invasion were not confined to the rank and file. Even the top dogs were potential security threats. Eisenhower himself was known to be having an affair with an Irish divorcee. Although Ireland was technically neutral, there was a lot of anti-British feeling in the Republic and, in the eyes of SHAEF, his indiscretion could leave him open to blackmail. Not surprisingly there were a lot of worried officers pacing the corridors of the invasion nerve centre when Eisenhower disappeared for some 'rest and recreation'.

Churchill was another potential security leak waiting to happen. He spent a lot of time on the telephone with American President Roosevelt and it was known that the enemy had the ability to intercept these calls. Although a new scrambling system was installed in early 1944, with the length and frequency of calls between the two after Christmas 1943, it wouldn't have taken a genius to figure out that something large and tasty was cooking in the Allied kitchen.

As D-Day approached, SHAEF, COSSAC, and the rest of the invasion team were getting more and more anxious. They were desperate to keep everything a secret from the enemy. Their already strained nerves were completely shredded when they started to see the code names of two of the proposed landing beaches: Omaha, Utah, as well as Overlord, Neptune (the code name given to the seaborne operation) and Mulberry (the name given to the huge temporary harbours needed for the invasion) were mentioned in Daily

Telegraph crosswords in May and early June 1944. Was this German intelligence leaking details of the invasion under their very noses?

Actually, no. MI5 got on the case and found a couple of school teachers, who had been doing the job for almost twenty years, composed the crosswords months in advance.

Despite many scares and numerous opportunities for the Germans to discover what was being planned, the invasion remained a secret.

The Grande Plan

The original invasion plan, devised by COSSAC in 1943, called for landings by three infantry divisions and two airborne divisions in Normandy. The naval requirements for such an undertaking were significant: over 3,300 landing craft of all shapes and sizes, over 450 warships of various designs, along with 150 minesweepers to clear a path to the beaches.

However, when SHAEF and Eisenhower got in on the planning act the first thing they did was widen out the invasion front to accommodate five infantry divisions; they also expanded the airborne role out to three divisions. The extra infantry divisions meant that the invasion front was widened out to the east to include the Cotentin peninsular, so that Cherbourg was reachable and the German reinforcements were stretched over a wider area. The also wanted to launch a second landing simultaneously in the Côte d'Azur region of southern France in an attempt to divert German troops away from the main landings in Germany. This second operation was called Anvil.

To make this new and improved plan a reality at least 1,000 more landing craft were needed. Britain had no more capacity to increase supply and much of the US Navy reserves of landing craft were being earmarked for work in the Pacific. There was still distrust in American ranks that the British wouldn't 'filter' some of the extra landing craft away for their own Mediterranean party as Churchill was convinced the 'soft underbelly of Europe' was there for the taking.

The bottom line was that the Americans didn't share the British view regarding the opportunity in the Mediterranean and the British were not backward in coming forward about their dislike for Anvil. The issue over Anvil and the Mediterranean was a cause of continuous tension during the build up to D-Day; the Americans clung on tightly to Anvil until mid-April 1945 when a compromise agreement was settled that Anvil would be launched to support Overlord, but not until 10 July. In the end, Anvil was renamed Dragoon and didn't actually take place until August.

Eventually, the basic objectives of the ground force were agreed; the American First Army, led by US Lieutenant General Omar Bradley, was to make an assault on two beaches with the main aim of cutting off Cherbourg and establishing the western flank of the overall Allied bridgehead. The British 50th and 3rd Divisions, ably supported by the Canadian 3rd Division as well as various armoured formations and Royal Marine Commandos, were to concentrate their efforts on the stretch of coastline between the River Orne and Port-en-Bessin. Their main objectives were the communication hubs of Bayeux and Caen.

Montgomery realised that both flanks of the seaborne landing would be vulnerable to enemy counter-attack, so he decided to use airborne troops, dropped into France hours before the invasion, in an attempt to secure these positions. The British 6th Airborne would be dropped to protect the Eastern flank and the American 101st and 82nd Airborne Divisions would be dropped in to the west.

The most easterly beach was code-named Utah and would be assaulted by the US 4 Infantry Division, followed by the 90th, 9th and 79th Divisions. Once the beach had been secured the forces would split into two, with one group making a bee-line for Cherbourg whilst another group headed south to cut off the peninsular. Bradley expected Cherbourg to be in American hands within a month.

Next door to Utah was Omaha. This beach was four miles long, had sheer cliffs at either end and in the middle was bristling with German armour. It was perhaps the most heavily defended beach out of all. The first troops ashore would be the US 1st Infantry Division, backed up by the 29th and 2nd Divisions. US Rangers had a special task; the capture of Pointe-du-Hoc, a vertical cliff which was home to a clutch of enormous naval guns perched on top that would have a large and uninterrupted field of fire on to the beach. The Rangers had to climb the cliff and knock out the guns. Fast.

Once off the beach the plan was to link up with British troops on their left at Port-en-Bessin and move south to secure a bridgehead.

The chaps at SHAEF knew that the troops going in to Omaha beach could potentially have a tough time of it; in an effort to help, an airborne attack was also planned in this sector. The 82nd US airborne would be dropped in and around the town of St Mère Église whilst the 101st would attempt to secure the beach exits and various bridges over the River Douve.

On the western flank of the invasion, the British and Canadian troops were earmarked to land on three separate beaches codenamed Sword, Juno and Gold over a twenty-four mile front. During the first wave only small sections of this twenty-four miles would be attacked, which meant these initial assaulting troops were isolated and in danger of losing touch with their comrades on either side. From Sword would be the main assault on to Caen, carried out by the British 3rd Division. This particular part of the line was very heavily fortified by the Germans, with the Orne estuary especially well defended. The 3rd Division would be assisted by men of the British 6th Airborne Division who were tasked to take the bridges over the River Orne, especially the bridges at Bénouville. This would severely hamper the enemy being able to bring up re-enforcements to the beach area. Another vital role for the 6th Airborne was to neutralise the formidable Merville gun battery that had many of the landing zones within its range and as such posed a huge threat to the invasion.

Three miles to the east of Sword was the Juno landing area. This would be a Canadian show with the 3rd Canadian Infantry Division going ashore first, helped by the 6th and 10th Canadian Armoured Regiments. They were also helped by some Royal Marine Commandos in an effort protect their flanks. Once ashore the Canadians were tasked to take the inland high ground immediately, as well as capturing the important Bayeux-Caen road and the airfield at Carpiquet, a few miles inland.

Finally, Gold beach was sandwiched in between the Canadians to the west and the Americans at Omaha in the east, it too was strongly fortified and for the assault Montgomery had chosen the British 50th (Northumbrian) Division. The Division had fought for Monty at Alamein, Tobruk Sicily and Italy and had objectives to occupy their stretch of the Bayeux-Caen road as well as link up with the American forces that had landed on Omaha.

There was no escaping it. This was a hugely ambitious invasion. The sheer scale and numbers involved made it similar to lifting up a sizeable city in England and moving it via small boats over to France, with enough supplies and resources to keep that city moving and living for weeks once they got there. The brunt of this logistical nightmare fell squarely into the lap of the Royal Navy. To be fair, the naval resource that was made available for D-Day was unprecedented in size and strength. Over 7,000 vessels of various size and shape were ready to bear down on the Normandy coast, either to deliver men, weapons and equipment, to clear mines to ensure a safe path to the beaches, or to blast seven bells out of the German defence systems. Whatever their personal objective, they were ready.

So too were the air boys. Approximately 11,500 aircraft were ready and willing to help smash any signs of German retaliation. This fleet included around 3,500 heavy bombers which would be used to destroy coastal defences and communication emplacements. There were also almost 4,000 fighters ready and primed to repel anything the Luftwaffe threw at them. Almost 1,500 transport planes would be used to drop paratroopers over enemy lines prior to the beach landings, plus 3,500 gliders which were vital in getting heavy equipment into the war zone.

In addition to this little lot, 500 reconnaissance planes would be buzzing high above the battlegrounds keeping an eye on the movements of German reinforcements behind the lines and relaying any decent information back to HQ. There was also another 1,000 planes earmarked for coastal reconnaissance looking out for U-boats in the Channel.

That was the plan. 156,000 infantrymen, 13,000 paratroopers and almost 200,000 naval personnel were all primed and ready to go.

It was to be the greatest amphibious operation in history.

Invention, innovation and invasion

Getting that many men, kit, vehicles, guns, ammunition and supplies across the sea and up the beaches was not an easy job, and would be impossible without a raft of specialised equipment. This was acknowledged by Churchill very early into the war. On 7 July 1940 he wrote:

"Let there be built great ships which can cast up on a beach in any weather large numbers of the heaviest tanks."

This would be the inception of the LST – Landing Ship Tank – one of, if not the, most important of all of the landing craft used for D-Day. Not only was the LST capable of carrying up to sixty tanks, but it could carry them across oceans and thus could be used anywhere on the planet, in any theatre of war. It was also able to sail directly on to a gently sloping beach so that its cargo of tanks can roll off directly on to land and into battle. To be able to do all of this was a marvel of design.

The LST's little brother was the LCT – Landing Craft Tank – which was a barge with an engine that possessed a wide opening bow door and ramp. It was able to carry up to five tanks directly on to the beaches, straight into battle.

The evil cousin of the LST was the LST-R, an adapted version of the Landing Ship Tank that boasted a bank of five inch rocket launchers to help smash coastal defences. It was also equipped with radar to help scan the coast for enemy movements. Developed by Colonel F.H.C. Langley of the Combined Operations Group these monsters were capable of firing over one thousand rockets in thirty seconds, equivalent to eighty cruisers. The firepower these LST-Rs were capable of was extreme and devastating; thirty-six were built for use in the Mediterranean and Normandy.

The fighting men were transported towards the invasion beaches in LCIs (Landing Craft Infantry) or LCA (Landing Craft Assault). LCIs were able to carry 200 men, where the smaller LCAs were capable of ferrying an infantry platoon of around thirty men directly on to the beaches.

Second only to the LSTs in its importance in the initial assault phase of the invasion was the D.U.K.W. amphibious truck. Known as 'ducks' by the infantry, these six-wheel vehicles were first produced in 1942 by GMC and based on a bog-standard US Army truck but heavily modified to be able to float like a boat when in the sea and drive like a normal truck when on dry land or the beaches. Its huge versatility and toughness made the D.U.K.W. a war winning vehicle in the eyes of many army senior officers.

Some of the most famous and iconic technical developments for D-Day were found on the British beaches and were there courtesy of Major-General Percy Hobart and the chaps in his 79th Armoured Division. A range of specialised vehicles were developed in an effort to get as many men and vehicles off the beaches in one piece as possible. They were nicknamed Hobart's Funnies although the task they carried out on D-Day was far from amusing.

Major-General Hobart was seen as something of a maverick and a liability by many of the British Army top brass. He ruffled too many feathers and had too many opinions on too many subjects for their liking. He was 'retired' in 1939 and when the Second World War kicked off in the autumn of that year, he was serving as a Corporal in the Chipping Norton Home Guard. Churchill, however, liked him and thought his vision and creativity could be a major asset to the war effort. In October 1940 he wrote to the Chief of the Imperial General Staff:

"The high commands of the Army are not a club. It is my duty...to make sure that exceptionally able men, even though not popular with their military contemporaries, are not prevented from giving service to the Crown."

That was that then. Hobart was back.

He was immediately thrown into leading a force of specialist combat vehicles, soon to become the 79th (experimental) Armoured Division. General Eisenhower quickly realised the usefulness of Hobart's work in developing his revolutionary vehicles and he personally made sure red tape was slashed and priority given to his requests. Hobart also happened to be Montgomery's brother-in-law and, although they didn't always agree on things, Montgomery always made sure Hobart's 79th Division had what they needed to get their job done.

One of Hobart's most remarkable achievements was the DD Tank (Duplex Drive) which was based on a normal Sherman tank modified with two propellers working off the main engine and a large watertight canvas screen which allowed the tank to float. Such tanks could be launched several miles off the invasion beach and be driven ashore. Once on dry land the screens were removed and the tank resumed normal operation, i.e. blasting the enemy to smithereens.

The DD Tank helped get ashore, but once on the beaches there were a whole new world of problems that Hobart had to try and fix. Those problems were called the Atlantic Wall. Churchill tanks were modified to carry a 40 foot long girder bridge to help get across tank barriers and over walls. The Crab, or Flail Tank, was specifically designed to clear a path through Rommel's beloved minefields. A huge metal drum fitted with long steel chains rotated at speed and thrashed the ground blowing up mines in its path in relative safety. It was crude, especially for the tank crew who had to deal with the noise and after-effects of continual mine explosions, but it was effective.

Other more destructive 'funnies' were the AVRE (Armoured Vehicle Royal Engineers) which was another modified Churchill tank that carried a powerful mortar that could fire large explosive shells over 150m with the express purpose of blowing enemy fortifications to pieces. The 18kg shell was nicknamed 'the flying dustbin'. Perhaps the most terrifying of all was the Crocodile; a Churchill tank that had its hull machine-gun fitment replaced by dirty great big flame thrower. The Crocodile could send a high pressure jet of flame and burning oil over 100m, it used so much fuel it needed its own 400 gallon petrol tanker which it towed behind. The Crocodile was a formidable weapon that was particularly good at clearing enemy bunkers, trenches, pill boxes and other fortifications.

By early 1944, Hobart had a brigade of each of the DD Tanks, Crab mine clearers and AVREs. He also had a smaller number of Crocodiles. The original plan was that the American forces would use a significant proportion of the funnies – indeed a third of the total production were offered to the US Army for use in the invasion. Despite Eisenhower liking the 'funnies', especially the DD Tank, take-up on the American side was minimal, mainly because many of these modifications were based on the Churchill tank and the Americans were not keen on adding another tank variation into their war inventory.

Cancellation, frustration and nerves

On 8 May the final date for D-Day was formally set by General Eisenhower. It would be Y plus 4. Y-Day was 1 June, this was the date when all preparations were to be completed and the Amy, Navy and Air Force would be all ready to go and give the enemy a good hiding. Therefore D-Day was set for 5 June 1944.

As May gave way to June it was finally time to get the men going and embarked on to their appointed ships for the Channel crossing. Slowly but surely the assault troops emerged from the barracks, tent cities and secure compounds and marched through towns and villages on their way to their embarkation sites. As the numbers of men, trucks, tanks, guns and other vehicles rumbling through the narrow streets steadily increased, the people of Britain started to sense the enormity of the situation.

Something big time was about to kick off.

The last days of May 1944 were hot. Very hot. Such intense heat didn't help the nerves, the stress and the tension levels amongst the men as they were jammed on to their ships like sardines and told to wait for the order to get going. They just wanted to get moving. On 1 June the first convoys set sail from more distant ports in an effort to reach their jumping off point on time. That night, the BBC broadcast twenty-eight cryptic messages to the French Resistance after the evening news, many of which were decoded by the Germans and put them on a more heightened sense of alert. The first tentative moves of the invasion were taking place but ultimately there was only one man who could press the 'go' button and that was Eisenhower, the Supreme Commander of Allied Forces. His was a difficult decision and could be ruined by one vital factor beyond his control.

The weather.

From 1 June the Commanders in Chief met with each other twice a day to pour over detailed weather reports. If the date of 5 June was to be kept they had to make the final decision by 3 June at the very latest. Churchill was also very nervous about the uncertain Channel weather and instructed his First Sea Lord to put the finest meteorological minds to figuring out if the invasion would be able to go ahead as planned. He demanded daily updates.

Meanwhile, the Germans were also keenly watching the weather. They were sure something heavy was imminent. On 3 June Rommel wrote in his daily report:

"Concentrated air attacks on the coastal defences between Dunkirk and Dieppe and on the ports strengthen the supposition that the main invasion effort will be made in that area...Since 1 June an increasing number of warning messages has been broadcast to the French Resistance..."

The weather had started to deteriorate significantly by this time and in Rommel's eyes the threat of imminent invasion seemed minimal at that moment. German naval experts were convinced the Allies needed five clear days to launch an invasion so Rommel took the opportunity to head to Paris to see his wife and also see Hitler to ask him to release some Panzer resources before the attack came.

Back at SHAEF the day of 3 June was a day of intense anxiety. The weather forecast for the next couple of days was not encouraging but despite the reports, more than in hope than anything else, Eisenhower gave orders for all advance units to prepare for a 5 June invasion. D-Day was on. For now at least.

The final weather conference was scheduled for 4am on the morning of 4 June. Convoys were forming up in open seas and final preparations were being made. The weather forecast for 5 June was bad; stormy and overcast with a cloud base of 500 feet and force 5 winds. Even worse was that the weather was deteriorating so quickly accurate forecasts for more that twenty-four hours in advance were almost impossible.

It was the cloud cover that worried Eisenhower the most. With low cloud it would be difficult, if not impossible, to guarantee air superiority over the invasion beaches. The naval bombardment would also be significantly hampered due to poor visibility. Ultimately Eisenhower was not willing to risk an invasion without the requisite air cover and at 0600 on the morning of 4 June he decided to put everything on hold for twenty-four hours.

Another weather meeting took place during the evening of 4 June. This time the meteorologists offered up a glimmer of hope. They anticipated a break in the storm, a window of thirty-six hours of relatively clear weather with only light winds. What's more, Allied bombers, fighters and spotters would be able to operate on the Monday night 5/6 June, although there would be scattered cloud. Eisenhower canvassed opinion from the rest of SHAEF, they were split as to whether to go. It was down to the Supreme Commander. He paced the meeting room in silence, all eyes following him. At 21:45 he gave his decision: *"I am quite positive that the order must be given."*

By 23:00 every vessel involved in the invasion had been given the order to resume operations. D-Day would be 6 June 1944.

Another weather meeting took place in the early hours of 5 June, the storm was still raging and the Allied top brass were getting nervous again. Where was this break in the weather? Despite this the meteorologists were even more convinced the break was going to happen before dawn. Ramsay and Montgomery were keen on going ahead, and after some considered thinking Eisenhower agreed. *"Okay. Let's go!"*

Operation Overlord was on.

Just six gliders: The pointy end of 156,000 men

Overlord was a risky operation there was no doubt. The brains of SHAEF had planned, re-planned and re-re-planned for every eventuality, and as a result the men going ashore on 6 June 1944 would be the most prepared invasion force in history. There was, however, one small issue that worried the planners. Actually there were many things that worried them; the beach defences, the monster enemy guns that looked down over the beaches, the hidden machine gun pits, the anti-personnel mines covering the beach exits, and of course the weather...but there was something else. Something potentially catastrophic.

The entire left flank of the invasion force was completely unprotected and at the mercy of the enemy's elite Panzer regiments. To the east of Sword beach lay significant amounts of German armour, and once they were given the green light, there was nothing to stop them pushing the Allied troops straight back into the sea. Something needed to be done to block the path of any enemy retaliation coming in from the east, otherwise it could all get very messy indeed.

In an effort to protect the eastern flank of Sword beach, the Allies wanted to capture the bridges over the River Dives using paratroopers, then get the paras to storm the two bridges that crossed over the Orne waterways (river and canal) at Ranville and Benoville. These bridges were the key routes out to the east and the only direct way the German armour could get into the fighting zone. Capturing these bridges would stop any German counter-attack dead in its tracks. The bridges, especially the two at Ranville and Benoville, would have to be captured intact; otherwise the paratroops in question would be trapped and isolated in enemy territory. Not a good thought.

The big question was this: were the paras the best group to get this job done? Sure, they could capture the bridges no problem, but would they be intact? An attack force dropped out of the sky would be relatively slow to organise once they had all landed. Getting everyone together and ready for fight would take up precious time, giving the Germans plenty of warning to organise their defences, blow the bridges and call for back up.

After careful consideration General Richard 'Windy' Gale, the Commander of the British 6th Airborne Division decided that the only way to capture the bridges intact was by deploying an assault group via glider. After consulting with Brigadier Hugh Kindersley, Commander of the 6th Airlanding Brigade he chose the men that would be used to take the bridges. The honour would fall to 'D' Company, 2nd (Airborne) Battalion, Oxford and Buckinghamshire Light Infantry under the command of Major John Howard.

On 2 May 1944 Howard was given his orders:

"Your task is to seize intact the bridges over the River Orne and canal at Bénoville and Ranville, and to hold them until relief..."

Operation Deadstick had been born.

During his May briefing, Howard was also told that the garrison holding the two bridges would consist of about fifty men armed with around half a dozen light machine-guns, a couple of anti-tank weapons and a heavy machine-gun that could cause a few problems if not taken out quickly. Also he should presume that the bridges would be primed and prepared for detonation. The proposed landing zone for the gliders was a small triangular shaped field no more than 500m long. The tip of the triangle was near to the south east end of the canal bridge and as such was a perfect jumping off point. As long as they landed in the correct place, taking the bridges shouldn't cause Howard and his men any major issues. The big problem would be fighting off any German counter-attack until the relief turned up.

That 'relief' would arrive in the form of the British 5th Para Brigade which would drop to the north-east of Ranville and immediately move to take up defensive positions around both bridges. At the same time, the British 3rd Para Brigade would drop south of Le Mesnil and as part of the seaborne landings, Lord Lovatt's Commandos would make a bee-line for the bridges as soon as they got ashore.

Local intelligence combined with numerous RAF reconnaissance sorties over the bridges suggested that the key defensive position in the bridge area was a pillbox that not only housed the heavy machine-gun but also the button to blow the bridges. Based on this knowledge Major Howard charged three men from his number one glider to knock seven bells out of that pill box immediately with grenades, while the rest of the men in the lead glider headed straight for the canal bridge. The men from number two glider would clear the defensive lines, trenches and any machine-gun posts from the east bank of the bridge while the chaps in number three glider would also get to the bridge in an effort to make it secure. For the river bridge, the instructions and tasks were the same for gliders four, five and six respectively.

After months of intensive training the small group of men from the Ox and Bucks Light Infantry were ready to give the Germans a kicking. On 3 June, during final preparations, Major Howard received a visit from Montgomery to discuss the upcoming adventure. Monty's final remark to Howards was as simple as it was poignant: *"Get as many of the chaps back as you can."*

At noon on 5 June Howard was given the green light to get moving. It was finally show time. As they climbed into their gliders each man grasped tightly to a rifle, a sten-gun or a bren-gun, half a dozen or so grenades, and copious amounts of ammunition. Some carried mortars and one man from each platoon had a wireless radio set. They all had blackened faces. They were ready. Major Howard visited every single platoon leader from each glider before finally returning to glider number one, shutting the door behind him. It was time.

At 2256 on 5 June 1944, a Halifax bomber of the RAF took off, it was towing glider number one. Five others followed suit a one minute intervals. Just after midnight the formation was flying low over the sea towards Caen. At 00:07 on 6 June the lead glider passed over the French coast, at this time they cut the ties to their bomber escort. They were on their own. These half a dozen gliders were the pointy end of 156,000 British, Canadian and American troops that were preparing to bear down on France by air and by sea.

The invasion had started.

Operation Deadstick: Pegasus Bridge

Major Howard had asked his pilot of number one glider to place the nose of the glider through the barbed wire entanglement towards to the top tip of the triangular landing area. That was a tough ask in daylight, but in the dead of night, with the stress and tension of the operation, this was a hugely improbable task. On its final approach the glider was coming in fast. Too fast. Pilot Jim Wallwork was forced to pull the parachute to slow them down, but despite this he managed to plant the nose of his Horsha glider smack in the middle of the barbed wire entanglement, exactly where Howard wanted. It was without doubt a remarkable piece of flying and Air Chief Marshall Leigh-Mallory called it the *"greatest feat of flying in the war"*.

However, it was not all flowers and cupcakes in glider number one. The impact on landing was a bit harsh to say the least and rendered most of the occupants momentarily unconscious. Not only that, both Wallwork and his co-pilot John Ainsworth were thrown clear of the cockpit and on to the ground. Technically they were the first Allied soldiers to touch French soil on D-Day. Albeit they were sparko.

Although the initial crash landing made an awful lot of noise, the German sentries in the area were not alerted. In the immediate seconds after the landing there was complete silence in the dark. They had managed to achieve complete surprise. The passengers of the glider quickly came to and started to organise themselves for the initial assault, as they were dashing towards their various targets glider number two landed.

In a matter of minutes after the first glider had landed grenades were being dropped in the machine-gun pillbox, clearing out all occupants, and specialist engineers were inspecting the bridge for explosives. Meanwhile Lieutenant Den Brotheridge emptied a full clip from his Sten-gun into one of the German sentries on the Bénoville Bridge – the first German casualty of the invasion. This gunfire aroused the rest of the defending garrison and a short firefight ensued, Brotheridge himself was hit in the back of the neck by enemy machine-gun fire and died a few hours later, the first Allied soldier to be killed by enemy action on D-Day.

By 00:21 the three glider crews had captured the canal bridge intact and had either killed or chased away practically all German resistance in the vicinity. It had taken just over ten minutes, but this initial success was not without cost. All three platoon leaders had either been killed or wounded.

Meanwhile over at Ranville, Lieutenant H.J. Sweeny and his platoon took the river bridge without even firing a shot.

Now all they had to do was to hold on until they were relieved.

Howard got busy finalising his defensive arrangements for both bridges. He was particularly worried by the situation towards the west end of the canal bridge. Beyond this point was a French countryside jam-packed with German troops, guns and tanks. Lots of tanks. Howard expected a rapid and vigorous counter-attack from the Germans at any given moment. He would not be disappointed. Almost immediately after he had finished positioning his men to defend the bridges, the clattering sound of tank tracks filled the air, then it appeared, approaching the west end of the canal bridge, just as he feared it would.

Howard's only anti-tank weapon, a single hand-held PIAT gun, had been positioned at the road junction in front of the western end of the canal bridge and was in the very capable hands of Sergeant Charles Thornton. He was the best PIAT handler in the group, and at this particular moment, he needed to live up to his reputation. He would have only one shot at the tank, and it needed to count, otherwise all of his mates positioned in and around the bridges would be in a whole world of trouble. Not only that, if those bridges were lost and regained by the enemy, the success of the entire invasion would be thrown into doubt.

No pressure then.

As the tank rumbled slowly around the T-junction to head up the road directly towards the bridge, Sergeant Thornton took careful aim and fired his PIAT...His reputation at being handy with this weapon was well founded, he scored a direct hit. BOOM!

The explosion from the tank was spectacular and provided quite a fireworks display that lasted well over an hour. It was sufficient to persuade the rest of the German counter-attack to fall back. The bridges were safe for the time being. For his handy work with the PIAT, Sergeant Thornton was awarded the Military Medal.

Back at the bridges, Howard gathered around his officers and ordered them to prepare for another counter-attack. Everyone was put on high alert ('Stand To!') until dawn.

When dawn broke, enemy sniper activity rendered any movement in and around the bridges very dangerous indeed. The Germans also sent up two gunboats and as they approached the area the lead boat started to let rip with its 20mm canon. It was PIAT time again. The PIAT was now in the hands of Corporal Godbolt and one well aimed PIAT bomb, which exploded inside the wheelhouse, was enough to put an end to that little party. All of the crew on the lead boat were either killed or taken prisoner. The second boat simply fled.

The Paras drop in

While the first glider troops were busy taking control of the two bridges, low flying Allied bombers were also in the area. They flew low over Ranville and they were bang on schedule. It was 00:50 and the Paras were coming.

Howard and his small group were part of the 6th British Airborne Division. Almost 7,000 British and Canadians were dropped into France on D-Day, along with over 13,000 paratroopers and 'glider-riders' from the US 82nd and 101st Airborne Divisions. They were tasked with securing both the east (British) and west (American) flanks of the invasion beaches before the main assault could take place.

A few minutes later Howard was blowing like a lunatic on a small metal whistle: Dot, Dot, Dot… Daa. It was a pre-arranged signal for the paras: V for Victory. Those men who were landing all around in the nearby fields knew that the bridges were in friendly hands and the shrill noise also acted as a good source of orientation. When the German tank blew up a bit later it too acted as the perfect homing beacon to the disorientated paras.

Strong winds and heavy German anti-aircraft fire had scattered the drop so much that only about 40% of the British paras were able to take an active role in the day's proceedings. That said, all of the British main objectives were successfully carried out and by 03:00 men of the 7th Parachute Battalion had arrived at the Orne River bridge to help out Major Howard's 'D' Company. All across the twenty-four square miles of drop zone, pockets of savage fighting broke out as scattered groups of paratroopers fought with German defenders in numerous isolated firefights. In this way hundreds of German troops were pinned down when they should have been trying to repel the seaborne invasion force.

Meanwhile, at about the same time as the exploding tank was giving the Allied troops a free fireworks show to the east of the canal bridge, Colonel Hans von Luck, Commander of the 125th Panzer Grenadier Regiment, received the first reports that British Paratroopers had had the gall and temerity to actually land in his patch. How very dare they! He immediately put his entire regiment on full alert and by 03:00 he was ready to kick the invaders back across the Channel.

Only he couldn't. He wasn't allowed to move a wheel without express permission from Hitler, and he was asleep. And no one was about to wake up the Fuhrer. No one. So, instead of launching a counter-attack of biblical proportions before the British could properly organise themselves and thus cutting off Howard and his men from the bulk of the paras, von Luck just had to sit and wait. He could do nothing until his Fuhrer woke up from his beauty sleep.

Frustrating or what?

The American airborne assault suffered a number of difficulties right from the off. Some 13,000 men were dropped by 822 aircraft; the pilots of these planes had a really tough job, made even worse by a big bank of low level cloud over the drop zone, and consistent German anti-aircraft fire. As a consequence, this air armada was rapidly scattered and the paras were largely dropped in the wrong places. Some landed in the sea, some landed in flooded rivers and marshland. Huge numbers of these men simply drowned under the heavy weight of their kit. Others hit trees or buildings. For those men dropping into France on that dark summer morning, the biggest danger wasn't a nasty German with a machine-gun, it was Mother Nature. Those that did manage to survive the initial drop were hopelessly lost and spent most of their first hours on French soil searching for their mates and avoiding German patrols.

Many men of the 505th Parachute Infantry Regiment (82nd Airborne Division) landed in and around the garrison town of Ste-Mére-Eglise. Paratrooper John Steele got his parachute caught on the spire of the town church and was forced to hang there 'playing dead' for over two hours while the battle for the town raged all around him. Eventually the Germans, who had been alerted by Allied bombings and the excitement of the locals, took him prisoner after repelling the initial attack. However, the Americans regrouped and took the town. By 04:30 the Stars and Stripes flag was flying over Ste-Mére-Eglise. It was the first French town to be liberated, but not without cost. By the end of the day the 82nd Airborne may have held the town, but was practically isolated and had 1,200 men that it couldn't account for.

The 101st Airborne faired slightly better. It too suffered heavy losses with only 2,500 men out of an original force of over 6,500 answering the roll call at the end of D-Day, but they had managed to seize many of their objectives including the vital beach exits at Utah beach.

In a funny way the inaccuracy of the parachute drop did a lot to confuse the enemy, as their reports on that morning gave no hint as to the actual targets and intentions of the Allied invaders. In the early hours of the invasion, both sides were scratching their heads wondering what to do next, but although both British and American drops were far from perfect, they both achieved their objectives.

Mission Impossible: Silencing the Merville Battery

The British 6th Airborne Division was having a busy morning. Not only were they involved in the capturing of the vital bridges over the Orne, they were also tasked with taking down the Merville Battery, situated a few miles inland on the east side of the river Orne, it was part of a cluster of redoubts that had been in that area for centuries, designed to protect the important estuary that took maritime traffic directly into Caen.

The Merville Battery was an absolute monster. In the run-up to the invasion it was believed that the garrison contained up to twenty separate gun-pits, each boasting three or four machine-guns as well as 20mm anti-aircraft guns. Then there was the small matter of the big guns. They were big. Really big. 155mm caliber naval guns to be precise, and that was enough firepower to pound the British landing zones almost three miles away. Therefore it was imperative those guns were silenced before a single Allied foot made it to the beach.

If all of this firepower wasn't bad enough, the battery was fortified and defended to the extreme. A 400 yard anti-tank ditch enveloped the north and west sides of the battery, this was fifteen feet wide and ten feet deep. Then there was the barbed wire. The outer ring wasn't too bad and would be possible to cut through, but the inner ring was a different proposition altogether. Six feet high and ten feet deep, this was a serious belt of wire. Then there were the mines. Thousands of mines were placed in between the wire belts and at various other places throughout the approach. With almost 200 soldiers garrisoned at the battery, the Germans were convinced it was impenetrable.

The task of knocking this monster out of action was given to the 9th Battalion, Parachute Regiment. Lucky things. In the months running up to D-Day they practised, practised, and practised some more. Honing, perfecting and finalising their assault plans.

Firstly, between 00:30 and 00:50 on the morning of D-Day, 100 Lancaster bombers would fly in attempt to soften up the target by bombing it to high heaven. There would be specially fitted out 'glider trains' that would bring in jeeps, anti-tank guns, flamethrowers, ladders, mine detectors and special 'Bangalore' torpedoes designed to cut through the barbed wire. The paras would be dropped about one and a quarter miles from the battery, with a smaller reconnaissance group going in first to check it all out, before the main assault team began jumping at around 00:50.

First to jump would be the taping party, which, using mine detectors, would clear a path through the mine field up to the perimeter fence and mark it out with tape. The rest of the assault group would follow (split into three companies: A, B and C). An hour and a half was put aside to reorganise once they had landed; they would set of to the pre-arranged 'base' which was about 500 yards away from the batter, at 02:35. The assault also consisted of three Horsa gliders that carried 'A Company' along with almost 600 engineers whose job it would be to destroy the guns with explosives. These gliders would have to land within the actual battery perimeter. Outside the battery the rest of the attackers would also get moving; 'B Company' would blow gaps in the wire and 'C Company' would carry out the main assault.

To some people, actually to many people, the plan seemed a bit suicidal, but the risks were worth taking as those guns could spell real trouble for thousands of British troops attempting to get ashore on Sword Beach. They had to give it a go. Indeed the Merville guns were deemed so dangerous to the landings that if the 9th Battalion could not knock out the guns, British naval gunfire would try to do it. That meant that the men of the 9th had to be well clear, regardless of the situation, by 05:30. Otherwise they would get caught up in some serious naval shelling. Timing was everything.

Leading this group of people was the Commander of the 9th Battalion, Lieutenant Colonel Terence Otway, and when he hit French soil and discovered that he had landed miles away from the rendezvous point, he was incandescent. He knew that his men must also be scattered about all over the place and, as he marched through the night in an effort to get to where he needed to be, he picked up numerous pockets of his men. Precious hours were being wasted and he was also very worried that his glider trains had also been scattered too. Without them, his chance of success was severely hampered.

As Otway finally arrived that the assembly point he realised that the first part of the plan had been less than fruitful. The bombing by the Lancasters had failed miserably, not one single bomb had hit its target. To add salt to the wounds, the precious glider trains had been lost at sea, that meant if the attack was to go ahead, it would have to make do without sufficient ammunition, without jeeps, without mortars, without anti-tank weapons, without lightweight foot-bridges, without machine-guns, without demolition equipment, without medical supplies, without an ambulance and without any real means of communication back to the seaborne army waiting just off the coast for news of success.

Bugger.

Otway counted up the men and resources he had available to him: 150 lightly armed men (instead of 750), a handful of medics, six Bangalore torpedoes (instead of sixty), a smattering of light machine-guns, a solitary Vickers machine-gun and a radio.

Double bugger.

Otway had a decision to make. He was woefully short of men and supplies to do the job, but the guns had to be taken out of action. The seaborne invasion forces were counting on them. There was not a doubt in his mind that they would push on and so he gave the order to move. It was 02:50 on 6 June 1944.

Otway put Major Alan Parry in charge of leading the main attack; they set off to cover the 2,500 yards to the outside perimeter fence where they would meet up with the reconnaissance and taping parties. The assault plan had been hastily revised to take into consideration their lack of men and resources. Two gaps in the wire would be cut through which four attack groups would advance, each attack group was responsible for taking out one of the big gun casements. The remainder of the Battalion would be held back as reserve. Because there were no tape or metal detectors, a path through the minefields had to be created manually, looking for each mine individually and making safe by hand. To mark a safe path they had to drag their feet to scratch out two lines in the earth.

Just as the Battalion were about to attack, two gliders appeared from out of nowhere, although there were no flares to illuminate the landing zone. One disappeared into the darkness, but one of them attempted to land on top of one of the casemates. It was being fired at by German anti-aircraft guns and soon the tail of the glider was on fire – there was no way it would be able to make any kind of landing on the casements itself. Bravely the pilot kept its course and ditched the glider into a nearby hedge.

Meanwhile, inside the battery, the Bangalore Torpedoes were detonated – the signal for the start of the attack. Lieutenant Colonel Otway screamed at his men, "Get in! Get In!" as the four assault groups made a bee-line for the two gaps in the wire and then on to the safe paths through the minefield. It was then that the German machine-guns opened up and all hell let loose. The darkness of the night was lit up by mine explosions, tracer bullets and grenades. All four assault group leaders were wounded but the paras pushed on, firing their Sten-guns from the hip at anything that moved. It was absolute chaos. Otway decided to throw his reserves into the fight too in an effort to keep the momentum of the attack going.

Each man had trained long and hard for this precise moment. Each one of them had a specific job to do and they were executing the game plan very nicely. Well placed grenades through doors and down ventilation pipes managed to quieten any defenders hiding within the casements, and after twenty minutes of hand-to-hand fighting, the last enemy machine-gun nest fell silent. Twenty-two enemy prisoners were captured and many more were killed, however large numbers simply hid out the way in underground dugouts. It was now time to turn their attention to the big guns themselves. Major Parry, despite a badly wounded leg, dragged himself round the guns, placing explosives into each breech, detonating the explosive and analysing the results. After knocking out the gun in casement 1, a large shell whistled past and exploded nearby, wounding Parry again, this time in the arm. The Germans were shelling the battery in an effort to rid it of its attackers.

Dawn was slowly breaking and Otway was preoccupied with how to get a message back to HMS Arethusa before she too started to bombard the battery. The naval gunfire observation party that had dropped with his men had failed to turn up. The only radio that survived the initial drop was also now dead. A yellow flare was found and lit and a pigeon was sent. There was nothing else to do but gather up the wounded and get well away from the battery.

HMS Arethusa did not open fire.

Only seventy five paras were still on their feet at the end of the assault. After a brief respite they were forced to move on to their next objective; to liberate the village of La Plein. Once they had moved out of the area, the Germans reoccupied the battery and although they were able to get two of the guns back working, the battery as a whole was nowhere near as effective as it could be. The actions of the 9th Battalion had undoubtedly saved many lives on Sword Beach that morning.

We will start the war from right here: Utah

Utah beach was the most westerly of the invasion beaches. It was approximately three miles long and had four main beach exits which the assaulting troops could use to get off the beach as quickly as possible and head inland. Exits one and two were towards the south end of the beach, whereas exits three and four were towards the north. The Army wanted to be dropped off opposite exit two, this was an area of beach that was only lightly defended and offered the best opportunity to get on and off the beach relatively quickly and safely. The Navy took one look at the beach and politely told their Infantry counterparts there was not a hope in hell of landing in that area. The low tide opposite exits one and two retreated out almost 1,000m, making the approach to the beach too shallow to get anywhere near it. No, the Navy would drop the men near exits three and four. No arguments.

Exits three and four were heavily defended and fortified. The low tide here reached out only 400m, and the general area was much more suited to an amphibious landing. The Navy knew it, the Army knew it, and so did the Germans. They had stuffed this part of the beach choc-full of big guns, small guns, obstacles and mines. If anyone was going to try and land on this beach it would be to the north, and they would be ready for them. You would have to be mad to try and land in the south.

The initial plan was to land the floating DD tanks first at about 06:30. There would be thirty-two of these tanks, carried forward by eight LCTs (Landing Craft Tanks). Right behind them would be twenty LCAs (Landing Craft Assault, better known as Higgins boats) each carrying a thirty man assault team from the 2nd Battalion, 8th US Infantry Division. A second wave of thirty-two LCAs carrying men from the 1st Battalion (plus engineers and demolition teams) would come in five minutes later. Wave three carried in more amour, including Sherman and Bulldozer tanks, and was planned for H plus fifteen minutes, a fourth wave would following a couple of minutes behind that lot.

All of these craft were due to be shown the way to the landing zones by three US Navy patrol boats. Unfortunately they had to leave one of the patrol boats back in England as it had damaged its propeller on its way out of port. That left just the two boats to show the way: PC-1261 and PC-1176. To be fair they were doing a good job of getting everyone to the right place at the right time – until PC-1261 hit a mine about five miles off shore and sank. It was about 05:55 and the Germans were beginning to wake up and throw shells at the approaching landing craft. Shortly after PC-1261 sank an LCT was also hit by a mine and sank immediately. It was starting to get chaotic.

With only one patrol craft in service many of the landing crafts were circling wondering where they needed to go. The sole remaining patrol craft decided that in the interest of time they would take the LCTs in as close to the beaches as possible and thus made a bee-line for the beach. It got the first wave of LCTs in as close as 3,000m (they were meant to have been launched at 5,000m). However, in the chaos of the moment and due to a strong current, they were actually pointing at the wrong sector of the beach.

The DD tanks in the LCTs were very slow to get ashore, so slow in fact that the drivers of the Higgins boats carrying the first assault wave got fed up and sped on past them. As such it was E Company of the 2nd Battalion, 8th Infantry Regiment, 4th Division that were the first Allied men to land ashore on D-Day. In that first wave was the assistant Divisional Commander of the 4th Infantry Division, Brigadier General Theodore Roosevelt Jnr, son of the former president and cousin of the current one. Roosevelt was fifty-six, had a heart condition and needed the aid of a stick to walk, but he insisted on going in with the first wave on the grounds that it would be good for the troops' morale.

As Roosevelt Jnr and his boys hit the beaches they encountered very little enemy resistance. The beach also didn't look like the topographical mock ups they had studied intensely back in England over the last few weeks. Roosevelt hastily consulted his maps with a group of his officers and realised they were in the wrong place. Instead of landing in the teeth of heavily fortified positions in front of beach exits three and four, they had actually landed some 1,000m further south. They were right opposite exit two, which, ironically, was where they wanted to be dropped off in the first place. On top of this piece of good luck, the enemy gun batteries that were in this part of the beach had taken such a pounding from the combined air and sea bombardments that only light rifle and small arms fire was being sent down on to the beach during the landings of the first wave.

Roosevelt had a decision to make. Should he attempt to move his entire landing force more than a mile up the coast and attempt to land in the correct place following the original plan or should he continue the landings at the current position? He had to make his mind up fast as some of the men were already advancing up the beach and crossing the seawall. It didn't take him long to make up his mind and he allegedly said, *"We'll start the war from right here."*

By the time the second wave approached the beach the Germans had finally woken up and started to hit the landing zones with 88mm shells, mortars and machine gun fire. Despite being under constant fire all day, Roosevelt repeatedly led his men up to and over the seawall and pointed them the way inland. His leadership, decisiveness and bravery on the beach that morning won him the Congressional Medal of Honor and also went a long way to ensuring the beach was secured within just three hours of the initial landings. By 11:10 they had joined up with the US 101st Airborne. Much of the area immediately inland from Utah beach had been flooded by the enemy and in an effort to reach their D-Day objectives many men found themselves waist deep in flood water, in many cases the water was over head height and the risk of drowning was very real.

The Utah landings were one of the major successes of the D-Day operations. The paras were crucial as they confused and occupied the enemy, preventing any significant counter-attack, and even though the original invasion plan had to be ripped up within minutes, the US 4th Division managed to take almost all of their objectives. In fifteen hours more than 20,000 men and 1,700 vehicles of various size and shape landed on Utah beach. Casualties were around 300.

All in all, a good day's work. However, a few miles down the coast on the next invasion beach the story was very different. That beach was code-named Omaha.

Bloody Omaha

To say that Omaha Beach was not the most ideal location for an amphibious landing is a massive understatement. It was a complete death-trap. The gently sloping beach of sand and shingle stretched over 7,000 yards up to large sandy 'bluffs' (mini cliffs that rose up to 30m in places). Due to the slight concave curve to the coastline these bluffs had a complete and dominant view over the entire landing zone. If this wasn't enough, strong offshore currents created sand banks and small valleys under the water that were exposed at low tide and created huge issues for the landing craft and vehicles trying to get ashore.

Then there was the small matter of German fortification.

The Germans had long since recognised the potential of this long and open stretch of beach as a likely invasion zone and had planned their regional coastal defences accordingly. Everything Rommel had learned during the First World War about stopping a full-on frontal assault he put into practice at Omaha. Thousands upon thousands of iron structures, wooden poles and jagged steel 'hedgehogs', many decorated with anti-tank mines or modified artillery shells, were planted up and down the beach from the low tide mark to the high tide point forming an almost impenetrable (and very explosive) defensive shield in front of the beach. The approach to the beaches would be a nightmare, and that's before any man even set foot on terra firma. If the attacking troops managed to weave a path through all of that little lot they faced a long journey over open beach; an open beach that was overlooked by steep bluffs that were brimming with firepower that would enjoy a clear and uninterrupted view of the entire beach, especially the five exits cut into the bluffs themselves. Rommel singled these exits out for special treatment, not only were they overlooked by numerous strong-points but each one was further reinforced with large concrete roadblocks and even more wire.

The overall strength of defensive power on Omaha was frightening: there were eight large concrete bunkers each containing heavy 88mm or 75mm guns, another sixty light artillery guns, thirty-five smaller artillery pieces, eighteen anti-tank guns and one central strongpoint housing flamethrowers. Running between all of these strongpoints and gun positions were miles of trenches concealing almost one hundred machine-guns. In case that wasn't enough, set back on top of the bluffs were numerous rocket launchers and mortar positions, ready and primed to blast the beaches to pieces. Last, but definitely not least, was the massive 155mm guns of the Maisey Battery, positioned on the western end of Omaha on top of a 100 foot cliff called Pointe du Hoc. Both Omaha and Utah beaches were within range of these monsters. There was not one single inch of that beach that wasn't under direct fire from a multitude of weapons.

Then there were the mines. Thousands of them were placed on the shingle embankment under the bluff and thousands more, along with assorted booby-traps and miles of barbed wire, were covering the exits off of the beach.

The task of landing on Omaha was handed to the men of the US 116th Regiment and the US 16th Infantry Regiment. They had been promised that a massive air and sea bombardment would smash the German defensive infrastructure to smithereens. They were also told that the German troops manning the beach defences were not top grade soldiers.

They would be disappointed.

The plan for Omaha was intricate and precise. H-Hour was set for 06:30 and as the first assault wave prepared for their journey to the beach the men bobbing up and down in their LCAs (Landing Craft Assault) heard wave upon wave of Allied heavy bombers heading inland to smash the beach to bits. Note that they only heard them. They didn't see them due to low lying cloud. Unfortunately, just as the men couldn't see the bombers, the bombers couldn't see their targets. They had to drop their bombs 'blind'. The crews were desperately trying to avoid bombing their own men and subsequently delayed the release of the bombs by a few seconds. As a result, 13,000 Allied bombs fell harmlessly inland. But they did make a complete mess of several acres of French farmland.

At H minus 40 minutes the battleships USS Texas and USS Arkansas launched an awe-inspiring bombardment onto the enemy strongpoints, but again due to low cloud it was very difficult to ascertain accuracy of fire and much of this naval fire missed its intended target.

The infantry attack would see the US 116th Regiment and the US 16th Regiment advancing side by side across what was in effect a four mile front. The first wave would consist of two battalions of each regiment as well as DD tanks, Navy underwater demolition teams and Army engineers. The demolition teams were tasked with blowing a path through the substantial underwater obstacle course, marking the safe path with flags so subsequent waves of landing craft would know where to safely drop off their fighting cargo. The frogmen had thirty minutes to complete this task before the second wave of landing craft were scheduled to arrive. After which, new assault teams, along with huge numbers of battle equipment such as tanks, jeeps, communication units, medical equipment, big guns, trucks etc. would arrive at the beach every ten minutes until 09:30.

By H-Hour plus 120 minutes the plan was that the invasion force would be driving out of the beach exits on their journey inland towards their D-Day objectives.

That was the plan but the plan failed. Big time.

Even before a single boot had set foot on Omaha Beach the plan was disintegrating. The air and naval bombardments had failed. The sea was rough, with waves up to six feet high, and the tidal currents were strong and messing with the positioning of the invasion force. By H-Hour, not only were most of the boats out of position, the men inside them were sick, cramped, wet and miserable. Many of them had been in their landing craft for more than four hours; they were exhausted before they had even fired a shot in anger.

At H minus fifty minutes (05:40) the DD tanks were launched 6,000 yards out from shore. Due to the rough seas most struggled to get going and only five of the thirty-two that were launched actually got to the beach. Between H minus ten and H minus five LCT(R)s (Landing Craft Tank with Rockets) started to fire thousands of rockets directly onto the beach, the plan was to smash the beach defences and keep German heads down. Unfortunately many of these rockets fell short and only managed to kill lots of fish.

The first landing craft hit Omaha Beach at H plus one. As they approached it was eerily quiet, some of the men could actually see the German defenders up on the bluff looking down at them but they were not firing. It was all a bit weird. Then, the ramp was lowered and all of hell was let loose.

In an instant, Omaha beach was transformed into a blazing inferno. Machine-gun fire slaughtered the men getting down the ramps. 'A' Company of the 116th US Infantry lost 96% of its effective fighting strength before any of them had fired a shot. By 06:40 (H plus ten minutes) only one officer of 'A' Company was still breathing. The story was the same elsewhere: the landing craft carrying the engineers was hit by mortar or shell fire with a result of 50% casualties and almost all of their kit lost. The demolition teams tasked with breaking a safe path through the water defences didn't stand a chance in the face of withering machine-gun fire, mortars, shells, and rockets. The landing craft carrying the HQ of the 743rd Tank Battalion was smashed as it approached the beach, killing everyone apart from a solitary officer.

The 16th US Infantry were getting a similar pasting, as described in one of their battlefield reports:

"As the landing craft reached the beach they were subjected to heavy artillery, mortar, machine-gun, and rifle fire, directed at them from pill-boxes and from the cliffs above the beach. Men were hit as they came down the ramps of the landing craft, and as they struggled landward through the obstacles, and many more were killed or injured by the mines attached to the beach obstacles. Landing craft kept coming in with their human cargoes despite the heavy fire and continued to disgorge them on to the narrow shale shelf from which no exits had been opened. Several landing craft were either sunk or severely damaged by direct artillery or by contact with enemy mines."

Hardly any man was able to cross the beach alive that morning, as more and more men were dropped off they simply crowded together at the water's edge, trying to find shelter behind the odd tank or bulldozer that had managed to get ashore, otherwise they hid between the dead bodies in an effort to become invisible to the enemy. At 08:30 the officer controlling the landing craft from the shore suspended any more landings because there was simply no space for any more men or vehicles. The situation was so bad that General Bradley seriously considered pulling out of Omaha and redirecting the rest of his men to land at Utah.

In a last throw of the dice, a number of naval destroyers, including the *USS Texas*, were maneuvered as close to the shore as was physically possible and they started to blast seven bells out of the bluffs at what was effectively point blank range. Slowly but surely, with the help of Allied air force spotters directing fire, one-by-one the German strong points were silenced. It was 11:00 and the tide was turning.

Small pockets of men formed impromptu assault groups and crawled out to neutralise pill boxes and machine-gun posts, and by 13:30 Bradley had received radio messages from the beach suggesting men were advancing up to the top of the bluffs.

Even though the Americans has a toe hold on the beach and the German resistance was fading, there were still pockets of fire that continued throughout the day, also the exists off the beach were heavily mined and booby-trapped. Progress was painfully slow. By the end of the day, the US infantry had managed to push inland just over a mile. Pockets of enemy resistance continued from within the Allied lines and the beach was fired upon continually. By 21:00 the planned infantry landings for D-Day was completed. 34,000 men had managed to get ashore, but not without loss. Casualties were in the region of 2,400, but it wasn't just the human loss that was startling that day; of the 2,400 tonnes of supplies that were scheduled to land, only 100 tonnes actually made it ashore in one piece.

La Pointe du Hoc

About five miles to the west of Omaha, a commanding piece of the coastline projected out to sea. The French called it La Pointe du Hoc, and this particular piece of coastline was nothing more than a sheer cliff, jutting one hundred feet directly up out of the sand, but on D-Day, this little piece of cliff was as important to the Americans as Pegasus Bridge and the Merville Battery were important to the British.

There were six reasons for the importance placed upon this cliff. Six 155mm naval cannons stolen from the French, each with a range of twelve miles. With this kind of firepower and range, not only could these guns cover both Omaha and Utah beaches, but they could also smash the Allied armada to pieces as it approached landfall. Naval and air bombardments pummeled the casements as best they could, indeed they had both been smashing it since May, dropping more than 10,000 tonnes of high explosives but they couldn't guarantee the guns were out of action and because of their position they couldn't be taken by paratroopers or gliders, therefore the guns had to be taken directly from the sea. If this wasn't tough enough, they had to be taken quickly to enable the safe approach and landing of the rest of the invasion force.

The cliffs were about one hundred feet tall. That doesn't sound particularly high; we're not exactly talking the Empire State Building here, but there was no direct way up and trying to scale a sheer cliff whilst hundreds of enemy soldiers are shooting you with machine-guns and also throwing bombs and grenades on your head would mean that the cliffs might as well have been the north face of the Eiger. It was an almost impossible job and it would take a very special group of men to even attempt such an assault.

Enter the 2nd Battalion, US Rangers.

Led by Colonel James E. Rudder, the US Rangers were some of the finest fighting men America had to offer. They had been training for this day for a very long time; they had been tucked away in Scotland with the British Royal Marine Commandos practising coastal assaults against cliffs. Nearer the invasion date, as they moves south to their embarkation points, they got some more practise in around Dorset and the Isle of Wight. They were fit, they were honed and they had a number of special gadgets to help them with their task, not least four amphibious DUKWS fitted with turntable ladders topped with machine-guns, fitted by the London Fire Brigade and ten LCAs (Landing Craft Assault) fitted with rockets that fired grappling hooks attached to rope ladders.

The plan was for three companies to assault the guns directly from the sea – a total force of just 255 men. They were to land at 06:30. Before the landings *USS Texas* would blast the cliffs to pieces for forty-five minutes, her guns would fall silent five minutes before the assault troops hit the beach. Another Ranger company – C company – was to land on the far right-hand edge of Omaha and move inland and follow the heavily fortified coastal road to join up with the rest of the Rangers at the gun position. Another two companies were held back in reserve, due to land at Pointe du Hoc at 07:30.

That was the plan, but just as with the main landings at Omaha, the plan had to be abandoned even before a shot had been fired.

At H minus forty minutes *USS Texas* opened fire at cliff and the gun positions and proceeded to blast the proverbial out of the position, lifting her fire as scheduled, five minutes before the first assault craft were due to hit the beach. The problem was, those first LCAs were heading in the wrong direction. In the pre-dawn light, a combination of navigational error and a strong current pushed the LCAs too far east and they were actually moving towards the Pointe de la Percée. By the time the error had been spotted and the boats turned around a DUKW and an LCA had been lost to enemy fire. The Rangers were down to 180 men before they even landed on the beach.

It was C Company who landed first. They were forty minutes late according to the plan, and their delay meant that they landed in broad daylight; also the delay meant that the German defenders had had plenty of time to get back to their positions after the naval bombardment.

When C Company hit the beach, the Germans were ready.

Of the sixty-eight Rangers from C Company only thirty-one made it to the base of the cliff. Nineteen men were dead, another eighteen were wounded and no-one in the Company had yet fired a shot in anger. Those men that managed to get to the cliff base were relatively safe for the time being; now all they had to do was climb the rocks. This was easier said than done as the DUKWs were not able to get close enough to use their ladders and many of the rocket propelled ropes/grappling hooks did not deploy properly because the ropes were too wet. In those first few minutes it was looking alarmingly similar to the situation unfolding over on Omaha. It was time for the Navy to save the day.

USS Satterlee and *HMS Talybont* drew as close to the coast line as they could and gave the Point everything they had. Combined with a last minute attack by a group of B-26 bombers, their fire was as accurate as it was deadly and forced the German defenders to take cover. This gave the Rangers a window of opportunity to scale the cliffs, which they duly took advantage of. By 07:45 all the surviving Rangers were on top of the cliff. Once there, the Rangers engaged the enemy in a fearsome firefight – the Germans were not about to give up their positions lightly. Eventually the enemy was subdued and the Rangers made a beeline for the gun emplacements.

The guns were not there.

In their place were telephone poles, the real guns had been moved in-land to protect them from the incessant Allied bombing that had taken place during the previous weeks. A patrol was sent out to find them, and by 09:00 they had been located in an orchard about 200 yards south of the batteries. They were all set up and ready to fire but there was not a German soldier in sight. The guns were quickly destroyed with a few well-placed thermite grenades.

The main objective of the US Rangers, to capture those guns, had now been completed; however the enemy had regrouped and started to put together a substantial counter-attack. The Rangers clung on and defended their gains doggedly despite running dangerously low on ammunition and supplies. They were eventually relieved on 8 June. Out of 225 men who landed on D-Day, 135 had become casualties, but they had got their guns.

Gold Beach

Every time I hear the word 'Gold' my son (7 years old at the time of writing) and I have the urge to break out into song:

> *Gold*
> *Always believe in your soul*
> *You've got the power to know*
> *You're indestructible*

Now, I am sure the men of the British 50th Infantry Division who had been tasked to assault Gold beach on 6 June 1944 would probably have a different reaction to the word Gold than me and my son. It is more likely they would recall the sound of shell, mortar, small arms and machine-gun fire rather than a bit of classic Spandau Ballet. And who can blame them, for although Gold beach was nothing like as fortified as Omaha, the British were not about to stroll up the beach and plant a flag. No, it would take a bit more than that to gain control of the beach.

Gold beach was smack in the middle of the five designated landing zones for the Allied invasion. Five miles wide and took in the coast towns of La Rivière and Le Hamel as well as the small port of Arromanches and the town of Longues-sur-Mer. Geographically it was a similar story to the other invasion centres; a large flat beach rising gently to either sand dunes or a sea wall on the edge of a village, and steep cliffs on each side of the beach. The Germans had done their usual in this area too; the beach was heavily sown with almost 2,500 obstacles and mines of various size and shape, there were also miles of barbed wire strung liberally around any potential exit routes, with yet more mines and booby-traps hidden to surprise any potential invader. Beach-side houses were turned into machine-gun strong-points and snipers nests, all arranged meticulously to give the defenders the best field of fire possible.

Then there were the big guns. And they were really big.

In late 1943 and early 1944 the cliffs at Les Longues between the Omaha and Gold beaches were a hive of construction activity as a monumental coastal battery was built to defend the coastline. When completed it boasted four 5.9 inch naval guns taken directly from decommissioned naval destroyers. They had an effective range of twelve miles and could fire directly upon Omaha, Gold and Juno beaches. The guns themselves were set back about 330m from the cliff edge, in a more forward position, close to the cliff edge itself was a two storey observation and fire control bunker complete with optical range, map room and accommodation. Telephone wires ran underground between the two sites; there were also underground passages and shelters.

All in all the battery was manned by 184 sailors, as well as the four monster naval guns there were six machine-gun pits, a mortar pit and an anti-aircraft gun provided some extra fire-power and protection. The clever people at SHAEF had obviously recognised the threat of the battery and in pre-invasion bombardments in late May and early June 1944 bomber formations dropped 150 tonnes of explosives directly on to the gun casements.

They didn't even make a dent.

The pleasure of capturing Gold beach was handed to the British 50th Infantry Division, facing them were a mixture of Russian conscripts and highly trained German soldiers, many of these defenders were positioned in houses along the coast which didn't offer the best protection from air and sea bombardments, but a potential ace up the Germans' sleeve was *Kampfgruppe Meyer*, an elite SS Panzer regiment, based in the nearby town of Bayeux that had practised rapid deployment to the coastal areas to repel an invasion. They had enough firepower to throw the Gold beach invasion force back into the sea.

H-Hour was set for 07:25 but before the first wave of assault troops hit the beach the Allied naval guns had their chance to put on a show. Within twenty minutes HMS Ajax had fired 114 shells and had succeeded in silencing the dangerous Les Longues battery. Coastal defences were smashed and because many of the German defenders had taken up positions in houses they were vulnerable to these attacks, a large number were completely destroyed.

The general plan was to first send in the assault engineers and Navy frogmen whose mission was to clear a path for the rest of the men through the mines and obstacles. Unfortunately the wind was whipping up an unusually high tide that morning, which meant almost all of the obstacles were still underwater. This, along with intense machine-gun fire from a number of strong defences, caused the engineers all manner of problems and they struggled to clear any kind of meaningful gap for the incoming landing craft. The strong tides also made launching the DD Tanks impossible. This meant the first wave of troops would be going in without artillery support.

Seven minutes later the first assault troops hit the beach. In that first wave were men from the 1st Battalion Royal Hampshire Regiment, as soon as the ramps went down in those first landing craft they started to take serious casualties. The Battalion's Commanding Officer and his second-in-command were killed within minutes from machine-gun fire. In those first critical moments the situation on Gold was bad – so bad, it looked like Omaha all over again.

The DD Tanks may not have been able to get ashore, but Hobart's 'Funnies' did make it and, although their beach clearing work was significantly hampered by the unusually high tides, they supported the infantry well. The 1st Hampshire's continued to encounter fierce opposition by the defending 352nd Division and wasn't able to capture the seaside village of Le Hamel until mid-afternoon. On the Hampshire's left flank, the 1st Dorset Regiment met with little resistance and had gained complete control of their sector within 1 hour and were quickly marching inland behind flail tanks that were proving very adept at clearing a safe path through minefields.

The other strong German defence position was at La Rivière on the eastern side of the beach. This position had escaped the worst of the naval and air bombing that had battered the other areas of the coast held up the advance but eventually surrendered during the late morning.

At mid-morning the Desert Rats of the 7th Armoured Division arrived, along with the 47th Royal Marine Commandos. These quickly took care of any isolated pockets of beach-side resistance and then joined the push inland towards the towns of Arromanches and Bayeux.

Meanwhile, back in Bayeux, General Kraiss, the commander of the German 352nd Division was confused. He had heard about large numbers of paratroopers being dropped near the Vier estuary (directly inland from Utah beach) and had mobilised his forces to deal with that threat. When news of a major landing at Gold beach reached him and he realised that Bayeux itself was under threat he had to waste several hours turning his men around. By the time they were ready to go in the right direction the opportunity for a swift and decisive counter-attack had passed. As a consequence advancing British troops managed to get to the edge of Bayeux by nightfall. The town was practically there for the taking and the Allies duly obliged the following day.

Almost 25,000 men had landed on Gold beach on D-Day with the loss of only 400 casualties. It was a truly remarkable achievement.

Gold
Always believe in your soul
You've got the power to know
You're indestructible

Payback Time: Juno

On Juno it was the Canadians' turn to get a taste of the invasion action. Many of the men of the Canadian 3rd Division who were chosen to assault Juno Beach on D-Day had already seen action in France; they had been involved in the disastrous 1942 Dieppe Raid, a raid that resulted in 3,623 Canadians dead, missing or wounded. That amounted to a 60% casualty rate and for the Canadians bobbing up and down in the landing craft just off of the June shore in the early hours of 6 June 1944, it was time for payback.

The six mile stretch of coastline that became known as Juno ran between Courseulles-sur-Mer and St Aubin and was sandwiched between the British beaches – Sword and Gold. In their infinite wisdom, the shiny brass of the *Kriegsmarine* (the Germany Navy) were convinced that heavy fortifications in this area were not worthwhile, predominately because of the large offshore rocks, exposed at low tide that protected the approach to the beach area. Despite this confidence, significant strongpoints were built in this area, especially around the small port of Courseulles and the towns of Langrune and St. Aubin which did not have the offshore rocks to protect them. There were twenty heavy and medium batteries facing the Canadians on that morning, along with the obligatory beach obstacles, and of course thousands upon thousands of mines.

Crucially only two of the fortified bunkers had actually been finished, the rest of the guns were housed in roofless bunkers or open gun pits. Also these strongpoints were not clustered close together, they were spread out often half a mile or so apart. Then there were the defenders themselves. The men designated to man the guns in this section were not exactly the cream of the crop; most were either under eighteen or over thirty-five and not regular soldiers. There were also some veterans of the Eastern Front who had been invalided out of front line action and to make up the numbers *Ost* Battalion troops from Poland, Russia and Soviet Georgia were also present. In total there were around 400 German defenders and they were about to face-off against 2,400 angry Canadians hell bent on revenge.

H-Hour was set for 07:35.

The night before, the RAF had led numerous bombing raids on the Juno defences, unfortunately very few bombs actually landed on their designated targets. At first light the USAAF took over to give the coastal defences a pounding but a combination of poor visibility and a fear of dropping their bombs on to the attacking troops meant they delayed dropping their bombs for a few vital seconds and as a consequence the majority dropped harmlessly inland.

It was then the turn of the Navy to smash the coast to pieces.

The naval bombardment started at 06:00 and looked impressive enough. However such massive firepower threw up so much smoke and debris that it was impossible to see if it was working or not. The bombardment finished at 07:30 – five minutes before the first wave was due to hit the beach, but because of the threat of the off shore rocks, it was decided to wait twenty minutes to give the approaching landing craft a bit more water clearance. This extra twenty minutes may have made it easier to get ashore, but it also gave the German defenders time to dust themselves down and get back to their guns.

The delay also meant that the strong sea current pushed the first wave of landing craft directly into a dense area of beach obstacles and underwater mines which caused chaos with many landing craft damaged or sunk due to mines on their final approach.

As the first ramps went down on the leading landing craft, enemy fire was conspicuous by its absence. It was very quiet. Perhaps the naval guns had done their job and smashed the defences to pieces? Maybe the German soldiers had all been killed or fled to safer positions?

Sadly, the answer was no on both fronts.

The enemy were there alright. They just had their guns trained on the beach, not the sea, and as soon as the first men waded ashore (many of them had to bail out of their landing craft early and waded in chest-high seas to get ashore) they let them have it. Big time.

In those first moments ashore, the Canadians took a bit of a pasting. Devastated by machine-gun and artillery fire, the men at the sharp end of the assault had a 50/50 chance of survival, and in those first few minutes, it was touch and go as to whether the landings would succeed. It wasn't until the DD tanks and other armoured Brigades started to arrive on the beach that some of the gun positions were silenced. Then, in the midst of the battle, with machine-guns, mortars and artillery shells all saturating the beach, the pipers of the Canadian Scottish Regiment started to play. They had played when the Regiment had set sail from England, they had played as they boarded their landing craft and nothing was going to stop them playing their pipes on the beach.

Within two hours Juno was secured and the push inland began. Fighting continued amongst the villages and streets, but only in St. Aubin were the Canadians really held up. There were so few German defenders in the area that there was simply no one available to put up any kind of resistance. By the end of the day the Nova Scotia Highlanders were just a few miles from Caen.

By night fall the Canadian 3rd Division had completely overrun the enemy garrison that defended their landing zone and had pushed in to France further and deeper than any other D-Day force. Casualties were not as high as had been anticipated, although they were still significant; out of the 21,400 men that were put ashore approximately 1,200 were casualties.

Despite this, the Canadians had avenged Dieppe at Juno Beach.

On! On! You noble English! Sword Beach

In the eyes of Montgomery, the landing zones on Sword beach were key. They were also some of the most dangerous areas of all of the landing zones.

Key, because a successful landing on Sword, the most easterly of the invasion beaches, would put the Allies within spitting distance of the strategically important city of Caen and the capture of Caen would go a long way to ensuring the Allies enjoyed a strong and stable foothold on the peninsula. Not only was Caen an important communications hub, its capture would also seriously slow any planned German counter-attack from the Pas de Calais region of France – an area teeming with panzer regiments that could cause the Allies no end of trouble if they got too close.

This threat of a full-on counter-attack by full size, battle hardened panzer regiments made Sword beach the most vulnerable too. This beach was closest to the enemy and would bear the brunt of any counter-attack. Added to this, the beach, although lightly defended in terms of coastal guns, when compared to Omaha still had enough coastal defences to cause any landing force an issue, plus it was surround by huge inland artillery positions such as the Merville battery and other large in-land batteries code-named 'Morris' and 'Hillman' each of which possessed more than enough fire power to smash the beach to pieces.

If this wasn't enough, off-shore rocks, along with the proximity of the Orne estuary and the town of Ouistreham, meant that the British 3rd Division, who were given the honour of assaulting Sword beach, would have to land on a very narrow front of just one brigade. Once ashore they were to make a bee-line for Caen. Their orders were explicit, by nightfall they were to have "captured or effectively masked" the city. Once this had been completed they were to link up with the 6th Airborne who would be holding on to the vital bridges over the Orne waterways. And they had to do all this whilst avoiding the 21st Panzer Division which was known to be in the area and within striking distance.

At 05:45 an impressive naval fleet of two battleships, five cruisers and thirteen destroyers opened up a ferocious bombardment on to the beach defences as well as a number of the inland batteries.

H-Hour was set for 07:25.

The DD tanks were scheduled to be first ashore, however, as on the other invasion beaches, they struggled in the high tides and strong currents and a number of LCTs and LCAs overtook them.
In that first wave was the landing craft housing the HQ of 'A' Company, 2nd East Yorkshire Regiment. Major C.K. King DSO tried to inspire his men down by reading extracts of Shakespeare's King Henry V over his crafts tannoy system:

"On! On! You noble English! Whose blood is fet from fathers of war-proof...Be copy now to men of grosser blood and teach them how to war!"

By 07:26 the first landing craft were hitting the beach. They were greeted by enemy machine-gun and mortar fire, not as bad as Omaha or Juno, but bad enough, thank you very much. As Royal Marine frogmen got busy on the beach obstacles and under-water mines, the first wave of infantry waded ashore. Casualties were heavy.

Immediately behind the first wave came the first section of LCTs carrying Sherman tanks and a multitude of Hobart's Funnies that immediately got to work clearing mines, breaking through barbed wire entanglements and bridging anti-tank ditches. Enemy fire from a number of isolated strong points continued to cause heavy casualties until a machine-gun platoon of the 2nd Middlesex Regiment landed and immediately got into the action with their heavy Vickers guns –not surprisingly, they made short work of the troublesome strong points. Within an hour or so most of the beach was secure; however in the area around Lion-sur-Mer the enemy continued to mount a stubborn resistance.

At 08:20 No 4 Commando landed on the beach opposite Lion-sur-Mer. Their target was to get to the Orne Bridges and meet up with the 6th Airborne. When the ramps went down they took immediate casualties. The Commandos were led by Brigadier Simon Fraser, the 15th Lord Lovat, a charismatic Highlander. In the chaos of the landings he ordered his personal piper, Bill Millin to start playing his pipes. Despite the risk of attracting enemy fire Millin duly obliged and proceeded to walk up and down the beach playing his heart out. Seemingly spurred on by the music, the Commandos quickly re-grouped and cleared the strong points that were causing them problems. They then split into two groups, one group went off in search of the Orne bridges whereas the other group headed for the heavily fortified positions of Riva Bella and Ouistreham. By 13:30 Piper Millin was playing his pipes once again, this time as he approached the Orne bridges.

Riva Bella and Ouistreham quickly became witness to intense house-to-house fighting as the Commandos, with the help of a number of DD tanks, slowly but surely pushed the enemy back.

By midday, Ouistreham was liberated.

Back on the beach the tide was coming in quickly and with the arrival of the 185th brigade it soon became very congested on the ever shrinking foreshore. Delays were inevitable as boats queued up off beach to deposit their vital cargo. The 185th were tasked with getting off the beach and on to Caen as quickly as possible, and although the leading elements of the brigade did manage to get as close as three miles from the perimeter of the city they were unable to progress any further.

Hot on the heels of the 185th came the 9th Brigade, they were ordered to move at once to the Orne bridges and prepare for a possible attack. The Panzers were on the move.

A battle group made up of forty PzKpfw IV tanks were motoring towards the coast, but unfortunately for them they ran into a strong defensive armoured force just west of the Hillman fortification. Despite sustaining significant losses, the Germans managed to squeak past and continue onto the coast, eventually reaching Lion-sur-Mer however ultimately it achieved little and did nothing to stop the Allied advance. The British 3rd Division had dealt with the only major D-Day counter-attack without too much of an issue.

By the end of the day the British had fallen just short of their original D-Day objective of taking the city of Caen, but they had managed to get almost 29,000 men ashore with just 630 casualties (killed, missing or wounded).

Not a bad day's work really.

Operation PLUTO (Pipeline Under The Ocean)

The Allied invasion force was perhaps the most mobile army that had ever been assembled. The idea was to land no less than 14,000 vehicles on to the D-Day beaches on the first day. By D-Day plus twelve there would be almost 100,000 Allied vehicles in France. Getting the trucks, tanks, jeeps etc. on to the beaches was one thing, but keeping them running as the advance progressed was a different problem altogether. Millions of gallons of fuel would be needed to keep the army mobile once they had landed. The bigwigs at SHAEF knew that, if their grand plan of Operation Overlord was to have any hope of success they needed to figure out how to supply the invasion force with a plentiful and constant supply of oil and fuel for their vehicles and machines.

The obvious way to get the required supplies across to where it was needed was to utilise a fleet of tankers, however these would be susceptible to enemy attack (by either U-boats or the *Luftwaffe*), as well as being dependent on the weather. No, they would not do. Another way was needed.

Way back in 1939 the idea of supplying fuel to the continent via an underwater pipe was already being discussed by a group of walking brains and during discussions in 1942 between the Chief of Combined Operations and the Petroleum Warfare Department, the concept of PLUTO was born.

PLUTO would be nothing less than a pipeline laid under the Channel that delivered fuel from the English coast directly to the beaches of France. This was easier said than done. Experiments in early 1943 with a pipeline across the Bristol Channel between Swansea and Ilfracombe proved a success but also revealed difficulties and issues with operation. It took much longer than anticipated to get a good seal on the various sections of pipe, and then the pipeline itself was damaged by the anchor of a passing tanker. It was 100 days before any fuel flowed through the pipe at 1,500 gallons per hour. A modest amount, but from small acorns mighty oaks do grow. Ultimately the brains behind PLUTO persevered with their idea of pumping millions of gallons of fuel under the ocean directly to France.

Over the next year or so the pipeline under the Bristol Channel actively supplied Devon and Cornwall with fuel, and allowed members of the RASC and Royal Engineers to train in preparation for D-Day.

Having large fuel storage facilities on the south coast would offer up too much of an easy target for the Luftwaffe, instead it would be safer to store a lot of the fuel in safer areas such as Liverpool and Bristol. This meant though, that before the Channel pipeline could be built, another pipeline was needed to get the fuel from these safer fuel storage areas down to the south of England ready for shipping across to France. Over 1,000 miles of pipeline was constructed at night to avoid enemy reconnaissance flights. As an extra step in trying to minimalise the risk of attacks on the various pumping stations and to preserve the secrecy of the operation, these were carefully disguised as bungalows, barns, gravel pits, garages and even an ice cream shop!

The main PLUTO operation consisted of over seventy miles of pipeline running from the Isle of Wight to the Cherbourg Peninsular. Construction started on 12th August 1944 and the first line was completed within a matter of weeks. However, the Allied forces were advancing quickly and almost immediately another

PLUTO was needed from the Kent coast to Boulogne. Another line was constructed and laid from the Kent town of Dungness to a beach on the outer harbour of Boulogne. The first line was laid in October 1944 with further lines laid over the coming months. In all over 500 miles of pipeline was laid under the Channel with the sole purpose of delivering fuel to the Allied war machine.

By January 1945 PLUTO was delivering 305 tonnes of fuel into France per day. By March this had increased ten-fold to 3,048 tonnes per day and eventually went on to deliver over 4,000 tonnes per day, equivalent to 1,000,000 gallons each and every day. That was enough to quench the thirst of even the greediest Sherman tank!

By VE Day, over 170 million gallons of fuel had been delivered to the Allied forces, it was, quite simply, an incredible feat of ingenuity and engineering. General Eisenhower described PLUTO in his report as, *"second in daring only to the artificial harbours projects."*

Mulberry: It's a harbour, Jim, but not as we know it

If the liberation of Europe was to be successful, the Allies would need more than fuel. They would need to be able to reinforce the initial landings with hundreds of thousands more men and vehicles, along with all the rations, ammunition, and supplies needed to keep the army advancing in good order. The only major port in the vicinity of the invasion beaches was Cherbourg and the Allies knew they couldn't guarantee this port would be of any use to them, they had to come up with a different solution.

On 30 May 1942 Churchill sent a note to Admiral Lord Louis Mountbatten, the Chief of Combined Operations:

> *Piers for use on the beaches*
> *CCO or deputy*
>
> *They must float up and down with the tide.*
> *The anchor problem must be mastered.*
> *Let me have the best solution worked out.*
> *Don't argue the matter. The difficulties will argue for themselves.*

In September 1943 the idea for a floating harbour was agreed and ratified by the Combined Chiefs of Staff. The specifications required were formidable to say the least. There would be two harbours built, codenamed Mulberrys. Mulberry A for the Americans would be positioned at St Laurent, whereas Mulberry B for the British would be positioned at Arromanches. Three weeks after the first wave of the invasion force had landed in France it was expected that each harbour needed to be capable of shifting 12,000 tonnes of cargo and 2,500 vehicles of varying size and design a day. It didn't matter which way they looked at it. That was a lot of 'stuff'.

Not only that, they will have to cope with the traffic of large ships, give shelter for landing craft in times of bad weather and do all of this for at least three months. Oh, and it had to ready and fully operational by 1 May 1944.

Mountbatten and his team in Combined Operations got together with some of the brightest engineering minds in Britain along with leading naval contractors and senior naval officers to come up with a solution. They had just seven months to design and build two artificial harbours, each one the size of Dover. It was time to get busy.

Many bright ideas were investigated but Mountbatten and his crew eventually settled on building breakwaters (codenamed Gooseberries) using sunken ships. About seventy ships would be used for each Mulberry. Intermingled within these ships were a number of huge boxes of concrete (known as Phoenixes), some of these the size of a three storey building. Once these concrete Phoenixes were fixed, floating roadways were put in position; these were made up of steel pontoon bridges (code-named Whales) that would be capable of moving in harmony with the twenty-three foot Normandy tide and enable supplies to get ashore with minimum fuss.

Dozens of construction companies all over Britain got to work making the necessary component parts. Various pieces of the Mulberry puzzle were hidden in coves, creeks and inlets around the coast, out of sight of prying enemy eyes, until it was time to ship them over to Normandy. The ships that were earmarked to be sunk and used as the breakwater were gathered in Scotland and one week before the invasion, set sail to meet up with the rest of the harbour jig-saw. To get the 600 pieces of Mulberry over to the Normandy coast required 200 tug boats, this was more than Britain had and numerous boats were requisitioned from the US.

The first blockships arrived in position under their own steam and were sunk on 7 June 1944. Among the blockships was the French battleship *Courbet* who was towed across the Channel. Half submerged and still flying the Tricolour, she was manned by French sailors and was used as an anti-aircraft position.

Mulberry B started to load trucks with supplies on 14 June, and the first tanks rolled off of Mulberry A just two days later. The harbours were up and working. A few days later the weather in the region turned ugly and the both Mulberry harbours were damaged. Although the American Mulberry A was damaged beyond repair, Mulberry B was quickly brought back into service and in one hundred days 2,500,000 men, 500,000 vehicles and 4,000,000 tonnes of equipment and rations were unloaded from its floating roadways. Eight months after it was built, it was still unloading supplies for the liberation of Europe.

Sit Rep: The end of the 'Longest Day'

Just after 9am General Eisenhower approved the release of a short, but important, news release:

> *"Under the command of General Eisenhower, Allied Naval Forces supported by strong Air Forces began landing Allied Armies this morning on the northern coast of France."*

As the Normandy sky darkened at about 22:00, the beach masters on all five of the landing zones started to pack up for the night. It had been a long day, but a successful one. Although there are no definitive statistics, it is estimated that over 130,000 men arrived from the sea, with another 22,000 dropping in from the skies.

When considering the fearsome reputation of the Atlantic Wall and the absolute audacity of wading into France from the sea in full view of the enemy, casualties were remarkably light. Secretly, many members of the Allied high brass were worried that this whole operation would be a disaster. Another Gallipoli. Mercifully, this wasn't the case.

Yes, there were casualties on all beaches and in all landing zones. The men that assaulted the beaches of Juno and Omaha suffered heavily, especially those in the first waves. However, casualty numbers for D-Day are estimated at 10,000 with around 2,500 killed, that's a 6.5% casualty rate and a 1.6% death rate. Under the circumstances these numbers are incredibly good.

From the British airborne troops on the east, to the American airborne troops in the west, the invasion front stretch out over fifty-five miles. But it was not one continuous line. Oh no. Between Utah and Omaha there was a gap more than ten miles wide, on the other side of Omaha, towards Gold there was another gap six miles wide. Between Juno and Sword there was another large gap; this time around three miles wide. In normal battlefield conditions, such gaps between armies would be catastrophic, but on D-Day they were largely meaningless. The Germans had no troops and no armour in the area to take advantage and with complete Allied air supremacy over the new frontline, any German attempt at moving significant resources into the area became very difficult indeed.

That said, from an ultimate objective point of view the results on D-Day were mixed. The British 6th Airborne had managed to do exactly what was asked of them. They had secured the bridges over the Orne waterways and held on until relieved, effectively securing the eastern flank of the offensive. On Sword beach the British had succeeded in getting off the beach, however they had been held up three miles from Caen, their ultimate D-Day objective. The strategically important airfield of Carpiquet, situated three miles to the west of Caen, was also not taken, although some Canadian troops had managed to reach the runways. Bayeux was still in enemy hands, although the British were only one and a half miles away and knocking loudly on the door. The story with the American part of the invasion was much the same. The Rangers had eventually found their guns near La Pointe du Hoc, but on Omaha the assault had struggled to secure any kind of toe hold inland, advancing just a mile. Even on Utah where the landings were much more peaceful the US 4th Division were still struggling to fully link up with the 101st and 82nd US Airborne Divisions, both of which had suffered badly during the last twenty-four hours. They were a long way off from effectively cutting off Cherbourg.

As night fell along the newly opened front, the Allied liberators started to organise themselves and dig rudimentary defensive positions. They had nothing else to do but sit and wait for the dreaded enemy counter-attack. To wait for the Panzers.

Mix-ups, egos and politics: Why Germany failed to push the invasion back into the sea

It had taken almost four years to build the Atlantic Wall. Four years of hard work and labour plus millions of tonnes of concrete, hundreds of thousands of re-enforcing steel rods, hundreds of miles of trenches, millions of mines and thousands of miles of barbed wire. Not to mention the thousands upon thousands of beach obstacles and booby traps on the beaches. It was without doubt a remarkable feat of engineering that sucked up huge resources and labour from the German war machine.

On Utah, Gold, Juno and Sword beaches it took the Allies about an hour before they had broken through the Atlantic Wall. On Omaha it took less than a day. Within twenty-four hours around 130,000 men had breached this fabled and seemingly impregnable defence structure.

There were three major problems with the Atlantic Wall: firstly it did not employ a 'defence in depth' strategy. Unlike the Hindenburg Line of the First World War the Atlantic Wall had no depth. Once you were through the initial line of static defences, bunkers, pill boxes and trenches you were in the clear. There was nothing else further inland to back it up. What's more, because the troops that manned the Atlantic Wall were forced to stay in their own positions, the men on either side of the invasion front were unable to come to the rescue. Finally there was the question of the troops themselves. It kind of makes sense to get captured Polish and Russian men to help build the fortifications and gun emplacements. But to ask them to wear a German uniform and fight to the bitter end was just fanciful thinking on the part of the Wehrmacht. It just wasn't ever going to happen. And it didn't.

Four years in the making. Twenty-four hours in the breaking. The Atlantic Wall simply wasn't all it was cracked up to be. Rommel was right. It was *Wolkenkuckucksheim*.

A less than effective Atlantic Wall wouldn't have been as catastrophic as it ended up being if the Germans had possessed a clear defensive strategy that was agreed upon and bought into by all of her commanders and officers. But there wasn't one. At all. Not even close.

Rommel was convinced the battle, and indeed the war, would be won and lost on the beaches and had said so publically on a number of occasions. Field Marshall von Rundstedt on the other hand preferred to use swift and powerful counter-attacks using the Panzers to push any invasion back into the sea. Hitler was unable to make a proper decision either way and in the end a messy compromise was agreed upon which, in the end, helped no-one. When it came down to it the officer class of the German Army let their men down badly. They were unable/unwilling/scared (pick which excuse you like from those) to make any decision on their own. They failed to take the initiative, failed to think on their feet in the heat of battle, failed to go with their instinct, failed to trust their training. Ultimately they failed to lead their men. Instead of taking the situation by the scruff of the neck they waited. They waited for orders from headquarters. Order given to them by some desk-bound staff officer who had no idea what was going on at the beaches. The Panzer commanders knew where their enemy was, they knew they were stronger, faster, harder than they were at that moment, they knew that if they acted fast they had a good chance of crushing the invasion before it gained momentum. But they couldn't move. They couldn't move because they didn't have the authority to give orders to their own men. Let me repeat that last one:

The Panzer commanders didn't have the authority to give orders to their own men.

Madness.

Where the Panzers were concerned, the go button could only be pressed by Hitler himself. And he was asleep. And no-one wakes the Fuhrer. Ever. So those Panzers just stood still and waited. Watching as the window of opportunity slammed shut right in their face.

The *Luftwaffe* was no better. Thousands of ships anchored off shore or moving slowly inland should have been an easy target for German bombers and fighters. The soldiers huddled on the beaches in those early hours would have been sitting ducks. But incredibly, during the whole day, just one single plane flew over the invasion armada. The opportunity was there for a concentrated bombing offensive. If it had happened early enough and with enough spite it may have made a big difference to the number of men and amount of supplies that could have made it ashore. Those German defenders manning the beach guns must have been cursing the *Luftwaffe* as they watched wave after wave of men wade ashore that morning. They must have cursed them every time the ground shook beneath them as a result of yet another Allied bombing raid...and all the time the King of the *Luftwaffe*, Hermann Goering, was too busy eating sausages at the Berchtesgaden with Hitler to really worry what was going on in Normandy.

The same could be said too of the *Kriegsmarine*. Again, the thousands of boats making up the invasion armada would have been easy prey for U-boats, but except for a small raid by three E-boats the *Kriegsmarine* did not make one single attack on the massed ranks of Allied shipping perched off the coast of Normandy. A golden opportunity simply sailed on by...

References, sources and further reading

Traditionally, the reference section of a history book is a neatly set out list of book titles, authors, publishers and publication dates.

Hopefully, as you have just read this Layman's Guide, you have realised that this is not like most traditional history books. These days the way we access information has changed beyond measure from how we did it just a few years ago. It won't be long when reference and source pages will just have one or two words: Google, Bing or perhaps another search engine of choice.

I have used the internet extensively in the research and composition of this Layman's Guide. There are a number of very decent websites that provides a great wealth of information on all aspects of D-Day:

Wikipedia is an obvious resource, although I have tried to double check all information I have used from this site with other resources. Wikipedia can sometimes mislead and misinform! Each of the invasion beaches have numerous dedicated websites, both official and unofficial, that are brim full of information, images, and videos. Generally www.6juin1944.com provides a great overview of the entire invasion zone, as does www.historylearningsite.co.uk www.dday-overlord.com and www.militaryhistoryonline.com For Omaha beach www.omaha-beach.org is a good resource as well as www.omaha-beach-memorial.org and www.omahabeach.org The other American beach was Utah and covering this particular landing zone is a brilliant website at http://www.utah-beach.com/

which just happens to be the official site of the beach museum in Normandy.

For Juno beach I recommend www.junobeach.org and http://members.shaw.ca/junobeach/ both sites give excellent details for anyone interested in what the Canadians went through on D-Day. From a British point of view the pick of the sites in my opinion include http://d-dayrevisited.co.uk/ and the website of the fabulous D-Day museum in Portsmouth: http://www.ddaymuseum.co.uk/

As well as the delights of the internet, I have of course used a plethora of written material in the research of this Layman's Guide. The heavyweights are there of course: Stephen E. Ambrose is the self-professed king of D-Day and I have used *Pegasus Bridge* (Pocket Books, 2002) and *D-Day* (Simon & Shuster, 1994). To complement the story of Operation Deadstick I can also recommend The Battleground Europe Title: *Pegasus Bridge and Horsa Bridge* by Carl Shilleto (Pen and Sword, 2010).

The Battleground Europe range of books also includes excellent reference works on all of the landing beaches and are well worth tracking down if you are after detail. A slightly different take on the invasion zone has been put together by Paul Reed with his excellent *Walking D-Day* (Pen and Sword, 2012).

Warren Tute, John Costello and Terry Hughes got together in the seventies to put together the remarkable book *D-Day* (Sidgwick and Jackson Ltd, 1974) and another vintage work of huge importance to the creation of this Layman's Guide was the epic *Bodyguard of Lies* by Anthony Cave Brown (Harper and Row, 1975) which covers the deception and secrets of D-Day to the nth degree.

More generic works of note include *D-Day, Dawn of Heroes* by Nigel Cawthorne (Selectabook Ltd, 2004), *Overlord: The Illustrated History of the D-Day Landings* by Ken Ford and Steven J. Zaloga (Osprey, 2009) and the truly incredible *Forgotten Voices of D-Day* by Roderick Bailey (Ebury Press, 2009).

No reference list on D-Day would be complete without a Sir Max Hastings double: firstly his revered *Overlord: D-Day and the Battle for Normandy 1944* (Pan Military Classics, 2010) closely followed by his more recent WW2 epic *All Hell Let Loose* (Harper Press 2012). Not to be outdone in the 'epic history telling' stakes is Anthony Beevor, his mammoth *D-Day: The Battle for Normandy* (Viking, 2009) is not for the faint hearted but does contain some golden snippets that make it all worthwhile.

From the other side of the wire I can recommend *Normandiefront* by Vince Milan and Bruce Conner (The History Press, 2012) as well as *WN62* by Hein Severloh, a German soldier who manned the guns overlooking Omaha Beach (H.E.K. Creative Verlag, 2011)

That lot should keep you busy for a while!

Final Thought

I really hope you liked this Layman's Guide. If you did, please take the time to leave a review on your local Amazon site. Nice reviews mean the world to me. If you didn't like it or think I can improve, then please drop me a line – you can contact me via my website on www.scottaddington.com I welcome all feedback, the only way I will improve as a writer is to listen to feedback.

Thanks once again!
Scott

About the Author

I am on a mission to write short, sharp history books that educate, entertain and inspire children, teenagers and adults who many not read 'traditional' history books very often.

I think we (and by 'we' I mean writers, broadcasters, historians, teachers, editors, journalists, tv producers and parents) have a great opportunity with the centenary of the First World War to educate and inspire our children to become interested in our history and understand what makes us who we are today. I try and write my books in an engaging way to appeal to those people who may have never read a history book before - hopefully after reading one of my books you might read a few more books on your new chosen subject!

My 'Layman's Guides' are perfect introductions to their given subject, I like to say that they are more like an informal chat over a cup of tea/coffee rather than a heavy and dull historical text. Currently I have three Layman's Guides published covering The First World War, D-Day and the Third Reich. More are planned including The Second World War, Waterloo and others!

The Great War 100 is my attempt to tell the story of The First World War using nothing but infographics. This is a brand new way of telling history, it has never been done this way before and I hope that this style of communicating complex information opens up the subject to many new people - especially children.

Follow me on twitter @scott_addington or subscribe to my newsletter at www.scottaddington.com - every new subscriber gets a free gift!

Printed in Great Britain
by Amazon

Want to know about D-Day and the Battle for Normandy without having to wade through thousands of pages? Want to know the facts and discover the who/what/why/when of Operation Overlord without being bored rigid? You have come to the right place!

D-Day: A Layman's Guide has been written specifically for readers who have little knowledge of D-Day and is designed to be the ideal introducton to a subject that can be quite daunting for many people.

More akin to a nice easy chat over a cup of tea than a heavy historical text, the story of D-Day and Operation Overlord flows naturally, albeit without mountains of minutae. This Layman's Guide provides enough detail to gain a good grounding of knowledge and understanding, without becoming overwhelmed in detail and complexity.

www.scottaddington.com

£2.50

ISBN 9781499349825